ILLUSTRATING PASCAL

Donald Alcock

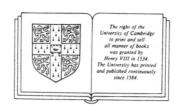

The right of the
University of Cambridge
to print and sell
all manner of books
was granted by
Henry VIII in 1534.
The University has printed
and published continuously
since 1584.

CAMBRIDGE UNIVERSITY PRESS

CAMBRIDGE
NEW YORK   PORT CHESTER
MELBOURNE   SYDNEY

CAMBRIDGE UNIVERSITY PRESS
Cambridge, New York, Melbourne, Madrid, Cape Town, Singapore, São Paulo

Cambridge University Press
The Edinburgh Building, Cambridge CB2 8RU, UK

Published in the United States of America by Cambridge University Press, New York

www.cambridge.org
Information on this title: www.cambridge.org/9780521336956

First published 1987
Reprinted 1990, 1991
Re-issued in this digitally printed version 2008

A catalogue record for this publication is available from the British Library

Library of Congress Cataloguing in Publication data
Alcock, Donald, 1930–
    Illustrating Pascal.
    Includes Index.
    1. PASCAL (Computer program language)   I. Title.
QA76.73.P2A38   1987   005.13'3   87–10369

ISBN 978-0-521-33695-6 paperback

Acknowledgements

This book was to have been a joint effort, first with Colin Day, then with Richard Kite. But despite all efforts the essentially personal nature of a hand-written book defeated every attempt at co-authorship. Nevertheless the present book is probably better for the experience. My warmest thanks to both of them.

My thanks also to Paul Shearing of *Euro Computer Systems Ltd.* for access to his firm's computers and helping me run my programs using Prospero's Pro Pascal and Borland's Turbo Pascal in addition to the Acorn ISO Pascal under which I had originally developed them.

Finally my thanks to my elder son Andrew for developing the program I employed to assemble and sort the index to this book.

CONTENTS

PREFACE

Pascal is a computer language which was designed by Professor Niklaus Wirth at Eidgnossische Technische Hochschule in Zurich. The first draft was completed in 1968. Since that time Pascal has become more and more popular, not only as a language for teaching principles of programming but also as a language in which to write complicated software.

This book introduces and demonstrates the whole of the language defined by BS 6192: *Specification for Computer programming language Pascal*, intended to be compatible with International Standards Institute standard ISO 7185. To keep in touch with reality I have run the programs in this book under three systems:

- ISO Pascal   by *Acornsoft*
- Pro Pascal   by *Prospero*
- Turbo Pascal   by *Borland International*

My style of presentation is pictorial. More can be conveyed by:

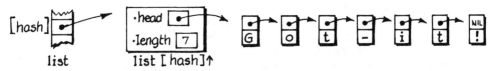

list   list [hash]↑

than by hundreds of words about hash addresses, pointers, records and linked lists. But I have been careful, too, about wording – aiming at simplicity and conciseness. The page layout has been arranged mainly as double-page spreads, each complete in itself, making it unnecessary to turn pages when referring to diagrams from text. With such layouts - and with diagrams being considered at least as important as text - the wording had to be fitted into place carefully. That is one reason for hand-written text; it is easier to use a pen than a type setter under such constraints. (With word processing and computer type setting making formal composition so easy the modern author is being seduced into thinking "How can I present this concept *without* a diagram?" when the question ought to be "How can I design a diagram to replace all these boring words?")

The contents of this book are organized as a programming-language manual. In chapter 1 is an example for the complete beginner, the aim being to demonstrate the concept of a stored program. In chapter 2 there is a quick canter through the rudiments of programming (variables, standard types, expressions, decisions and loops) which should be easy going for those who have written programs in other languages. These two chapters cover enough ground to present each feature of Pascal in the context of a complete program.

Chapter 3 is short but important; it defines the notation used through-out the rest of the book for describing the syntax of Pascal statements and forms. This notation is a blend of Backus-Naur form and railway-track diagrams. It does, I believe, convey structure at a glance — and with no loss of rigour.

From chapter 4 onwards each facility of Pascal is introduced in the context of a working program. The longer programs serve not only to demonstrate facilities of Pascal but also to illustrate fundamental techniques of programming — Quicksort, recursion, rings, binary trees and hashing being among them.

My biggest headache was dealing with interactive input. Pascal was designed in the days of card decks and magnetic tapes; the logic of Pascal's WRITE and READ statements did not allow for programs prompting their users for data from the keyboard. Nowadays such interaction is taken for granted — the reader of this book would probably expect to run the examples interactively — but unfortunately the problem has been solved differently in different versions of Pascal. So I have provided the examples with the simplest possible input statements and noted where the reader who has an interactive system should include prompts for the convenience of the program's user. And I have devoted a short chapter (chapter 11) to the prob-lems one can meet on trying to use Pascal interactively.

If at first you find the punctuation of Pascal programs fussy,
    and
        find
            yourself
                lurching
                    towards
                        the
                            right
                                margin,
don't despair; you soon grow accustomed to it. When you discover *records* the sun begins to shine again. When you reach *pointers* (and can make *chains* and *stacks* and *rings* and *trees*) you will become addicted. There is no known cure for addiction to Pascal.

REIGATE

Surrey, U.K.

Donald Alcock,

November 1986

1

PRINCIPLES

THE CONCEPT
INTO PASCAL
TYPING
COMPILATION
STEPS TO EXECUTION

THE CONCEPT

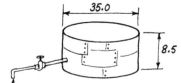

OF A "PROGRAM" ≈ SKIP THIS UNLESS YOU ARE COMPLETELY NEW TO COMPUTING

Assume there is no computer to help solve this problem confronting a painter; how many pots of paint are needed to paint the roof and wall of this oil tank?

The paint manufacturer says each pot has enough paint to cover an area of 236.0

Recall that the area of a circle is given by πr^2 (where r is its radius) or $\pi d^2 \div 4$ (where d is its diameter). Recall also that the circumference of a circle is given by πd (where d is its diameter as before). So the painter can work out:

$$\text{AREA OF TOP} = 3.14 \times 35.0^2 \div 4 = 961.63$$

$$\text{AREA OF WALL} = 3.14 \times 35.0 \times 8.5 = 934.15$$

The area to be painted is the sum of the above two areas. Into this area must be divided the coverage of a pot of paint so as to give the number of pots required:

$$\text{POTS} = (961.63 + 934.51) \div 236 = 8.03$$

A number with a fractional part like this is called a *REAL*. Because you cannot readily buy a fraction of a pot of paint the *REAL* must be rounded up to the nearest whole number, or *INTEGER*. To do this *truncate* the *REAL* and add 1:

$$\text{FULL POTS} = 8.03 \; +1 = 9$$

the solution

If the dimensions had been such that the number of pots worked out at 8.00 instead of 8.03 the solution would still be 9 pots. This is not arithmetically precise but would make the painter feel happier than an answer of 8.

Now suppose the painter wanted to set down this calculation in a general way such that if the problem arose again he would have only to substitute a few numbers and "turn the handle" for the new result to fall out.

Name some little boxes for holding numbers. The *contents* of each box will vary from problem to problem.

coverage

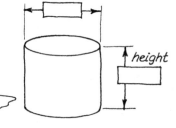

diameter

height

Don't forget to draw and name the boxes needed to store intermediate results:

top   wall   pots   fullpots *for whole numbers*

pi

3.14

read only

Put an approximate value of π into a special box. This value remains constant regardless of oil tank and paint pot ≈ hence the padlock.

A list of instructions ≈ called a program ≈ could be named and written as illustrated below:

PROGRAM painter (*INPUT* some data, *OUTPUT* results);

CONSTANTS   pi = 3.14 { *to be used, not changed* }; *declare the names of all boxes to be used, and the types of value to be contained*

VARIABLES   diameter, height, coverage, top, wall, pots, fullpots, these boxes are for REALS, but fullpots *is a box for an* INTEGER ;

locked boxes *unlocked boxes*

BEGINNING OF THE SET OF INSTRUCTIONS

✳ *from a waiting line of data,* READ *numbers into boxes:* diameter, height, coverage ;

✳ *into box* top *put the result of: the number from box* pi *times the* SQUARE *of the number from box* diameter, *divided by 4.0;*

✳ *into box* wall *put the result of: the number from box* pi, *times the number from box* diameter, *times the number from box* height;

✳ *into box* pots *put the sum of the numbers found in boxes* top *and* wall *after dividing this sum by the number found in box* coverage;

✳ *into box* fullpots *put the result of* TRUNCATING *the number from box* pots *and adding* 1;

✳ WRITE *a note to the painter (* 'YOU NEED', *write here the number found in box* fullpots, ' POTS' *)*

END OF THE SET OF INSTRUCTIONS .

If you had the waiting line of data:

| 35.0 | 8.5 | 236.0 |

and were to obey the program above (being a human computer) you would go through the calculation set out opposite and end by writing the following note to the painter:

YOU NEED 9 POTS

Of course if you had a *different* line of data you would get a *different* result.   That is the essence of a "program" ≈ it is a generalized calculation.

3

INTO PASCAL

The English instructions on the previous page would be too wordy to be used as computer instructions. Nevertheless the English may be translated into Pascal without losing the original sense.

First of all the recurring phrase " *the number from box ...* " may be treated as understood. For example the third instruction of the program may be shortened to:

> ✫　　*into box* wall *put the result of* pi *times diameter times* height ;

Then do without the phrase " *into box* such and such *put the result of...* " by abbreviating to the name of the box followed by a symbol thus:

> ✫　　wall :=

where := may be pronounced " becomes " when the statement is read aloud.

Now replace the word " *times* " by an asterisk. Similarly, replace " *add* " and " *subtract* " by plus and minus signs; replace " *divide* " by a slash 《 its formal name is *solidus* 》. Thus the third instruction may be shortened to:

> ✫　　wall := pi * diameter * height

which reads aloud " wall *becomes* pi *times* diameter *times* height ".

There are other abbreviations in Pascal, and some important rules of punctuation to be explained later, but the stage is sufficiently set to illustrate a program in Pascal:

```
PROGRAM   painter ( INPUT,  OUTPUT );

   CONST  pi = 3.14 ;                              declarations
   VAR    diameter, height, coverage, top, wall,
          pots: REAL;   fullpots: INTEGER;

BEGIN                                              separators

   READ ( diameter, height, coverage );           instructions
   top := pi * SQR ( diameter ) / 4.0 ;
   wall := pi * diameter * height;                 SQR() and TRUNC()
   pots := ( top + wall ) / coverage ;            are functions; Pascal
   fullpots := TRUNC( pots ) + 1;                  provides a selection
   WRITE ( 'YOU NEED', fullpots, ' POTS' )         of these
END .
```

Compare this program with the English one. The declarations and instructions show a one-to-one correspondence.

The mixture of capital letters and small letters is explained later.

TYPING

The keyboard of a popular home computer is sketched below; other keyboards are similar.

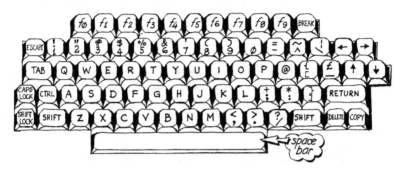

The keyboard on a VDU connected to a time-sharing computer would look similar to that above. There is always a key at the right, engraved with the word ENTER or RETURN or the symbol ⏎. Pressing this key causes a fresh line to be started. Every keyboard has letters A to Z, digits 0 to 9, full stop, comma, colon, semicolon and the arithmetical symbols + − * / needed for the present example.

Before starting to type you have to "enter the editor" and the way to do this depends on the installation. Using Acornsoft Pascal on the BBC Model B you type EDIT and press RETURN . Using Pro Pascal you use the local editor or a word processor such as Word Star. Using Turbo Pascal you press E .

Once "inside" the editor type fearlessly, taking care over the punctuation which, in Pascal, is pernickety. There is always a way to backspace and re-type a wrong character; on the BBC Model B press DELETE , on some other keyboards press DEL or BACKSPACE .

Other editing facilities differ greatly from installation to installation. The Turbo Pascal editor is modelled on the word processor called Word Star. Every editor is horrible when you first try it but appears to improve as you grow accustomed to it. Patience and perseverance.

Ignore the distinction between capital letters and small letters; type with or without the CAPS LOCK key having been pressed. The only line of the example in which this makes any difference is:

```
write ('You need', fullpots, ' pots')
```

where the phrases between apostrophes reappear in the result precisely as typed in the program; upper case, lower case or mixture as above.

Whilst typing the program notice that the computer does not *obey* any of the instructions. The computer, at this stage, is not even aware that a Pascal program is being typed; it knows only that a *file* is being typed. You could type Twinkle, twinkle little star in Portuguese and there would be no objection from the computer.

5

COMPILATION

AND, THE PROBLEM OF ENTERING DATA FROM THE KEYBOARD ...

A Pascal program cannot be set to work simply by entering RUN as with many BASIC systems; a Pascal program must first be *compiled*. Compilation means translating the *source program* from Pascal into an *object program* encoded in the computer's own language. When a Pascal program is put to work it is the object program that is obeyed, not the source program.

After compilation you have two versions of the same program; one in Pascal and one in machine code ((or something close to it)). If you were able to display the object program on the screen it would appear to be gibberish.

Pascal runs faster than BASIC because the object program is in machine code which can be obeyed directly or in a code which can be interpreted efficiently. By contrast, statements of a BASIC program are interpreted from source. The price of faster execution is the time and inconvenience of compilation. However, on most installations it is possible to save object programs, hence re-run programs without recompiling them. This course is followed by the steps depicted opposite where a copy of the compiled program is saved on disk.

The steps depicted opposite go from typing a program to running it. Down the left of the page are *commands* typed at the keyboard to initiate each step. The commands are particular to the installation, those shown being imaginary but typical. MYSOURCE and MYOBJECT are assumed to be names invented by the programmer.

The final step depicted opposite assumes INPUT comes from the keyboard and OUTPUT goes to the screen. This arrangement is typical today but is by no means the only way to run Pascal programs. The language was designed at a time when files were saved on magnetic tape, INPUT came from a deck of punched cards, OUTPUT went to a line printer. To make a Pascal program send prompts to a screen and read data from a keyboard requires a suitably modified compiler. If you have such a compiler there should be no difficulty in running the examples in this book. But if prompts and responses get out of sequence ((questions following answers)) refer to chapter 11 which explains the logical difficulties and their diagnosis. It may be that your compiler cannot compile an interactive program properly ⇌ in which case you may still run the examples in this book but with data waiting on a disk file rather than being typed at the keyboard when the program has been set running. This *batch mode* arrangement is depicted below:

GO

data on INPUT file on disk

You need 9 pots

OUTPUT

"BATCH MODE"

STEPS TO EXECUTION

Commands to the operating system vary from one installation to another but the process depicted in steps below is typical:

EDIT

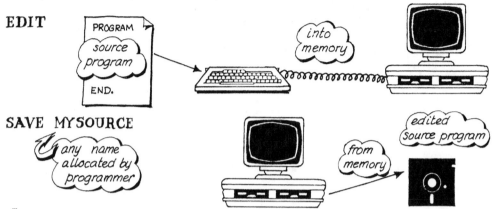

PROGRAM
source
program
END.

into memory

SAVE MYSOURCE

any name allocated by programmer

from memory

edited source program

Assume that the program, when run, would expect data from the keyboard. If it expected data from a disk file it would be necessary at this stage to type, edit and save a file of data in the same manner as depicted above for saving the source program.

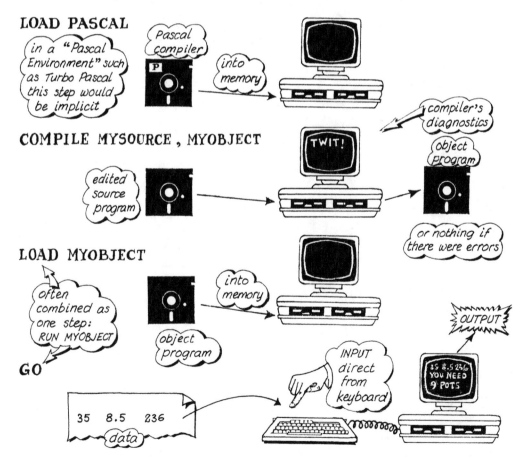

LOAD PASCAL

in a "Pascal Environment" such as Turbo Pascal this step would be implicit

Pascal compiler

into memory

COMPILE MYSOURCE , MYOBJECT

edited source program

TWIT!

compiler's diagnostics

object program

or nothing if there were errors

LOAD MYOBJECT

often combined as one step: RUN MYOBJECT

GO

object program

into memory

INPUT direct from keyboard

35 8.5 236

OUTPUT

35 8.5 236
YOU NEED
9 POTS

data

7

EXERCISES

1. Implement the oil-tank program. This exercise demands using the editor and submitting a program for compilation. Getting to grips with a new system is always troublesome; this exercise is probably the most difficult in the whole of this book.

2

RUDIMENTS

PUNCTUATION

A typical Pascal program has the following skeleton:

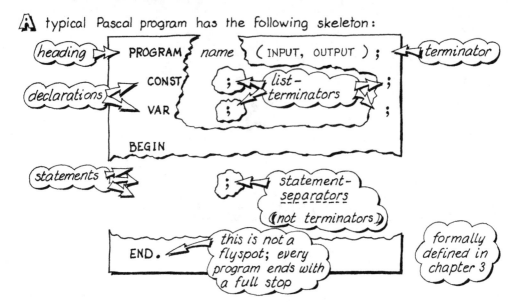

The heading is *terminated* with a semicolon.

Every list in every declaration is *terminated* with a semicolon.

Statements are *separated* from each other by semicolons.

The words BEGIN and END are not statements, they are effectively punctuation marks. BEGIN behaves as a left bracket and END as a right bracket. Because they act as punctuation marks a semicolon after BEGIN or before END would be redundant. BEGIN and END are much used in Pascal programs to make *compound* statements, where a compound statement (depicted below) is one that may be employed wherever a simple statement would otherwise be allowed. An example is:

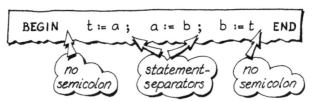

Words in other statements act as punctuation marks too. None of these has yet been demonstrated but here is an example:

Because statements are separated by punctuation marks the layout of a program on the page is not important to the compiler. Two rules are enough to satisfy the compiler:

- Don't run words together:

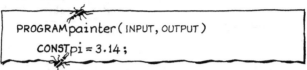

```
PROGRAMpainter ( INPUT, OUTPUT )
    CONSTpi = 3.14 ;
```

- Don't break up a single item with spaces or new lines:

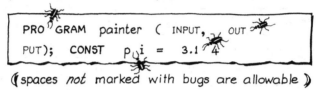

```
PRO GRAM  painter  (  INPUT,   OUT
PUT);  CONST   p i  =   3.1 4
```

《 spaces *not* marked with bugs are allowable 》

Although layout is not important to the compiler it is vital to the programmer's understanding. The introductory example illustrated the use of *indentation* to clarify the structure of a program. No specific rules for indentation are given in this book; the principles are conveyed by example. But if the examples in this book were to be run on an installation offering *automatic* indentation the resulting patterns would probably differ from mine. Ideas about the ideal layout differ, but all agree that indentation should make the structure of a program as comprehensible as possible. 《 Glance forward to page 17 to see a much-indented program. 》

The words PROGRAM, CONST, VAR, BEGIN, END 《 and thirty more, yet to be introduced 》 are called *reserved words*. Never extend a reserved word:

```
        CONSTANT                  VARI
```

and never try to shorten a reserved word:

```
        PROG    painting ( INPUT, OUTPUT );
```

Use capital letters or lower-case letters or a mixture of both. This book employs a mixture for reasons explained later.

| PROGRAM PAINTER(INPUT,OUTPUT); | program painter(input,output); | Program PAINTER(INput,OUTput); |

But in *strings* there is a distinction between them:

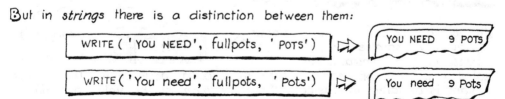

```
WRITE ( 'YOU NEED', fullpots, ' POTS')   ⇒   YOU NEED   9 POTS

WRITE ( 'You need', fullpots, ' Pots')   ⇒   You need   9 Pots
```

Make names as long as you like but ensure that every name is unique as far as the first eight characters. Some compilers would treat NUMBEROFMEN and NUMBEROFWOMEN as the same name.

VARIABLES

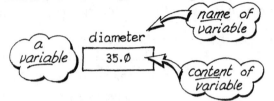

A SIMPLE VARIABLE TO ILLUSTRATE THE CONCEPT OF VARIABLES GENERALLY

The unlocked little boxes of the introductory example are called *variables*. A simple variable is a conceptual box having a *name* and a *content*.

A variable is created in the computer as a result of declaring it in a VAR statement. The declaration specifies both the name of that variable and the type of its content. Type is further discussed opposite.

```
VAR  diameter: REAL;
```

The symbol compounded of a colon and equals sign ≈ pronounced "becomes" ≈ signifies that a value (typically the result of evaluating an expression) is to be assigned to the box.

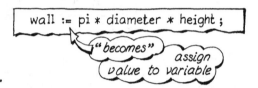

```
wall := pi * diameter * height;
```

In the introductory example the contents of variables do not change; each has a number assigned to it and there the number stays. But the program could be modified to use fewer variables. In the following version there are several assignments to variable x:

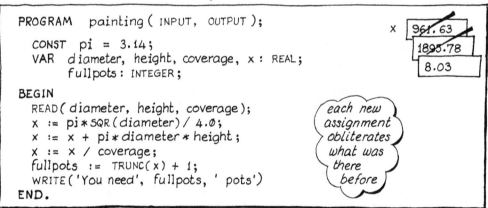

```
PROGRAM  painting ( INPUT, OUTPUT );

   CONST pi = 3.14;
   VAR  diameter, height, coverage, x : REAL;
        fullpots : INTEGER;

BEGIN
   READ( diameter, height, coverage );
   x := pi * SQR (diameter) / 4.0;
   x := x + pi * diameter * height;
   x := x / coverage;
   fullpots := TRUNC( x ) + 1;
   WRITE ('You need', fullpots, ' pots')
END.
```

x 961.63
   1895.78
   8.03

each new assignment obliterates what was there before

CONSTANTS

A SIMPLE NAMED CONSTANT TO ILLUSTRATE THE CONCEPT

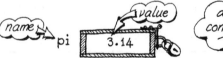

The locked little box of the introductory example is called a *constant*. Such constants are created as a result of declaring them in a CONST declaration. The *type* of constant is declared intrinsically from the *form* of the value put into the box. The decimal point in 3.14, for example, shows that pi names a REAL constant.

```
CONST pi = 3.14;
```

notice the equals sign; not :=

12

STANDARD TYPES

Integers are whole numbers ≈ negative, zero or positive:

no decimal point

- **constants** of type INTEGER must all be declared as here ➥

> CONST   dozen = 12 , decr = -1 ;

- **variables** of type INTEGER must all be declared as here ➥

> VAR   i, j, k : INTEGER;

- an **expression** assigned to an integer variable must reduce to an integral value; this precludes divisions of the form i/j as explained later

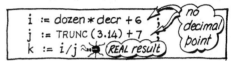

> i := dozen * decr + 6 ;
> j := TRUNC (3.14) + 7 ;
> k := i/j   *(REAL result)*

no decimal point

Reals are numbers with a fractional part. A real may be negative, zero or positive:

- **constants** of type REAL must all be declared as here ➥

decimal points essential

> CONST pi=3.1415926 , couple=2.0 ;

- **variables** of type REAL must all be declared as here ➥

> VAR x, y, z: REAL;

or 180

- an **expression** assigned to a real variable may reduce to a real or integer value; Integer values are automatically converted to reals before assignment. (Mix-

> x := pi / 180.0;   *(REAL result)*
> y := i/j;   *(auto. conversion*
> z := i + 2   *from int. to real)*

tures of real & integer terms in an expression are allowed: implications described overleaf.)

Characters are letters, digits and symbols; type CHAR means single characters:

- **constants** of type CHAR must all be declared between apostrophes ➥

> CONST p='A', q= '*', r = '6';

- **variables** of type CHAR must all be declared as here ➥

> VAR a, b, c : CHAR;

- characters may be compared, the result being Boolean, the basis of comparison being *ordinal* value: 'A' < 'B', 'B'<'c' etc. and '0'< '1', '1'< '2' etc.

> IF (p>a) AND (c ='X') THEN

Boolean values are *false* or *true*. (In Pascal, *false* is "less than" *true*.)

- Boolean **constants** are supplied, needing no declaration by programmer

FALSE X   TRUE ✓

- Boolean **variables** must all be declared as here ➥

> VAR ok, alive : BOOLEAN;

- a Boolean **expression** must reduce to the value *true* or *false*

> IF a=b THEN ok := TRUE;
> IF alive AND ok THEN WRITE('Great!')

13

EXPRESSIONS

The introductory example illustrates numerical expressions in assignment statements. Here are two of them:

```
pots := ( top + wall )/ coverage;          ← real assignment
fullpots := TRUNC ( pots) + 1;             ← integer assignment
```

Brackets ensure the desired order of evaluation. If brackets were omitted from the first of the examples above:

pots := top + wall / coverage ;

the division would be done first. Division has higher precedence than addition. In numerical expressions the precedence is:

higher	*	/
lower	+	-

← * and / have equal precedence
← + and - have equal precedence

The second of the assignments above illustrates an assignment to an integer variable. The function TRUNC( ) delivers an integer result, the 1 is written without a decimal point, so the two terms sum to an integer value. In general, when all terms have integer values the expression itself reduces to an integer value.

There is an important exception to the rule stated above. A division (using the slash) always delivers a real result:

$$6.5 / 2 \rightarrow 3.25 \quad (real)$$
$$6 / 2 \rightarrow 3.0 \quad (real: N.B.)$$

Integer division ⇌ quotient and remainder ⇌ may be achieved using the operators **DIV** and **MOD** as explained later.

An expression may comprise a mixture of integer and real terms. The presence of one real term, or of one slash, is enough to make the resulting value real. TRUNC( ) or ROUND( ) may be used to convert a real term to an integer term.

The function SQR( ) raises the value in brackets to the power 2, but there is no *operator* (such as ↑ in BASIC) for raising to any power. This is done by taking logarithms as shown opposite. Non-mathematicians should take it on trust that A↑X in BASIC may be expressed as EXP(LN(A) * X) in Pascal.

It may seem strange to some, but > and <= etc. may be used as operators too. 1>2 has the value *false* and 1+2 = 3 *true*. Expressions which contain such operators reduce to Boolean values and are called Boolean expressions or *conditions*. Boolean expressions may contain the *logical operators* NOT, AND, OR, and also terms of type CHAR:

```
ok := ( 1 = 2) OR ( ch >= 'A' );
IF ok THEN
```

The monthly repayment, m, on a mortgage loan of s pounds over n years at p percent compound interest is given by ⇒

$$m = \frac{sr(1 + r)^n}{12\,((1+r)^n - 1\,)}$$

where $r = p \div 100$

Here is a program to work out m, given values for s, p and n.

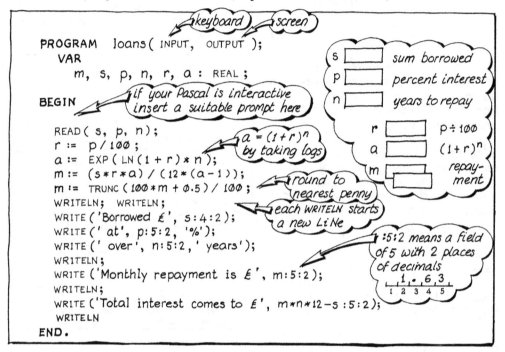

```
keyboard    screen
PROGRAM   loans( INPUT,  OUTPUT );
   VAR
      m, s, p, n, r, a : REAL ;
   BEGIN           if your Pascal is interactive
                   insert a suitable prompt here
      READ ( s, p, n );
      r := p / 100 ;           a = (1 + r)^n
      a := EXP ( LN(1 + r) * n );    by taking logs
      m := (s * r * a) / (12 * (a - 1 ));
      m := TRUNC ( 100 * m + 0.5 ) / 100 ;    round to
                                              nearest penny
      WRITELN;  WRITELN;              each WRITELN starts
      WRITE ('Borrowed £', s:4:2);   a new LiNe
      WRITE (' at', p:5:2, '%');
      WRITE (' over', n:5:2, ' years');
      WRITELN;
      WRITE ('Monthly repayment is £', m:5:2);
      WRITELN;
      WRITE ('Total interest comes to £', m*n*12-s :5:2);
      WRITELN
   END.
```

s ⬜ sum borrowed
p ⬜ percent interest
n ⬜ years to repay

r ⬜ p ÷ 100
a ⬜ (1 + r)^n
m ⬜ repayment

:5:2 means a field of 5 with 2 places of decimals
  1 . 6 3
  1 2 3 4 5

The screen, at the end of a run, should look like this:

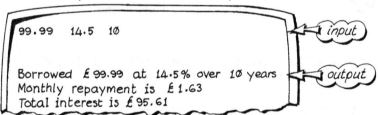

```
99.99   14.5   10            input


Borrowed £ 99.99 at 14.5% over 10 years    output
Monthly repayment is £ 1.63
Total interest is £ 95.61
```

If your version of Pascal permits interactive working, insert a WRITE statement before READ so as to make the screen prompt for the data needed.

The above program does nothing to check data. If the user of the program entered a wrongly-formed number (perhaps letter O in place of digit 0) the program would fail. Most programs in this book are equally lax in this respect.   The reason for the laxity is that checking data thoroughly would make the programs too long for their purpose ≈ which is to illustrate succinctly various other aspects of programming. It is left as an exercise to make these programs friendly and "robust".

DECISIONS

A program may be made to do different things according to outcome. Here is a trivial example ➡

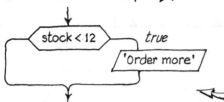

IF stock < 12 THEN WRITELN ('Order more');

The stock < 12 is a Boolean expression; its value is either *true* or *false*. If the value of stock < 12 reduces to *false* then the WRITELN statement is not obeyed; control would simply pass to the next statement.

In general the IF statement permits any number of statements to be obeyed according to whether the value of a Boolean expression proves to be *true* or *false*. ➡

The conditions illustrated here are no more than a comparison of two terms. Conditions may be more complicated, involving the logical operators AND, OR, NOT. For example

(initial >= 'E') AND (initial < 'L')

where 'initial' is a variable of type CHAR and holds the initial letter of a surname. A result of *true* would mean that the surname belonged in the E to K telephone directory.

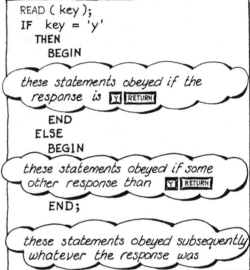

```
READ ( key );
IF  key = 'y'
    THEN
        BEGIN
```
these statements obeyed if the response is [Y] [RETURN]
```
        END
    ELSE
        BEGIN
```
these statements obeyed if some other response than [Y] [RETURN]
```
        END;
```
these statements obeyed subsequently whatever the response was

```
keen := ( x = y ) OR ( z >= 3 );

IF  NOT keen THEN
```

The value of a Boolean expression may be assigned to a Boolean variable and subsequently tested.

FIELDS

Field width and number of decimal places may be specified after a colon as shown below:

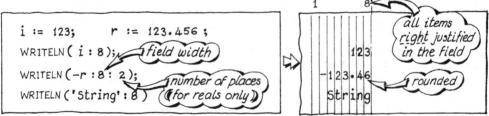

```
i := 123;       r := 123.456 ;

WRITELN ( i : 8 );          field width

WRITELN ( -r : 8 : 2 );     number of places
                            (for reals only)
WRITELN ('String' : 8 )
```

1   8

```
                    123
          -123.46
          String
```

all items right justified in the field

rounded

You can plot curves by making field-width an *expression* as demonstrated later.

SHAPES

Here is the flow chart of a program designed to compute the area of a geometrical shape: rectangle, triangle or circle.

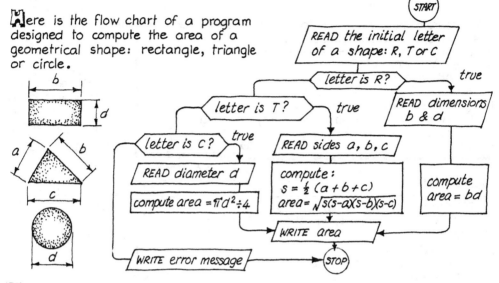

Here is a program to reflect the flowchart:

```
PROGRAM  shapes( INPUT, OUTPUT );
    CONST
      pi = 3.1415926 ;
    VAR
      letter : CHAR;    s, area, a, b, c, d: REAL ; ok: BOOLEAN;
BEGIN
    ok :=   TRUE ;
    READ ( letter );
    IF (letter = 'R') OR (letter = 'r')
      THEN
          BEGIN
            READ ( b, d );
            area := b * d
          END
      ELSE  IF (letter = 'T') OR (letter = 't')
          THEN
            BEGIN
              READ( a, b, c );
              s := 0.5 * (a + b + c);
              area :=  SQRT( s*(s-a)*(s-b)*(s-c))
            END
          ELSE  IF (letter = 'C') OR (letter = 'c')
            THEN
              BEGIN
                READ (d);
                area := pi * SQR(d)/4
              END
            ELSE  ok := FALSE;
    IF  ok THEN  WRITE ('Area is ', area:8:2) ELSE  WRITE('Must be R or T or C')
END.
```

INPUT

OUTPUT

R 3 4
Area is 12.00

write the number in a field of 8 with 2 decimals

Area is   .
        1 2 3 4 5 6 7 8

17

LOOPS

A program may be made to go back and obey a sequence of instructions several times over:

```
PROGRAM   xmas ( OUTPUT );
   VAR  humbug: INTEGER;
BEGIN
   FOR  humbug := 1 TO 3 DO
      WRITELN ( 'We wish you a merry Christmas');
      WRITELN ( 'And a happy new year')
END.
```

this statement obeyed when humbug contains 1, when humbug contains 2, and when humbug contains 3

this WRITELN obeyed once, after loop is finished

More usefully:

```
PROGRAM   tables ( INPUT, OUTPUT );
   VAR valu, product, multiplier: INTEGER;
BEGIN
   READ ( valu );
   FOR multiplier := 1 TO 10 DO
      BEGIN
         product := multiplier * valu ;
         WRITELN ( multiplier:2,' *', valu:2, ' =',product:4)
      END
END.
```

Note: WRITELN ('something') is equivalent to WRITE ('something'); WRITELN

BEGIN and END are "brackets" enclosing the compound statement which follows DO

If the outcome of the above trivial programs is not immediately obvious they should be tried out before reading on. Looping is fundamental to programming.

The FOR loop is called "deterministic" because the number of times round is determined before looping starts. Not so the REPEAT loop. The following fragment could be substituted between the outer BEGIN and END. above:

```
READ ( valu );
multiplier := 1;
REPEAT
   product := multiplier * valu ;
   WRITELN (multiplier:2,' *', valu:2, ' =', product:4 );
   multiplier := multiplier + 1
UNTIL multiplier > 10
```

adjustment within the loop

more appropriate applications of the REPEAT loop given later

The FOR loop and REPEAT loop are executed at least once (unless something goes so wrong that they are not executed at all). But there is also a loop for which the test for execution is made at the start, the loop being skipped over if the test fails :

```
READ ( valu );
multiplier := 1;
WHILE multiplier <= 10  DO
   BEGIN
      product := multiplier * valu ;
      WRITELN ( multiplier:2,' *', valu:2,' =', product:4);
      multiplier := multiplier + 1
   END
```

skip over when multiplier > 10

more appropriate applications of the WHILE loop given later

OLD GLORY

In 1912 "Old Glory", the American flag, had 48 stars (one per state of the Union) and 13 stripes (one per original Colony). The program below displays a rough approximation to Old Glory c. 1912. Nowadays there are more states, hence more stars.

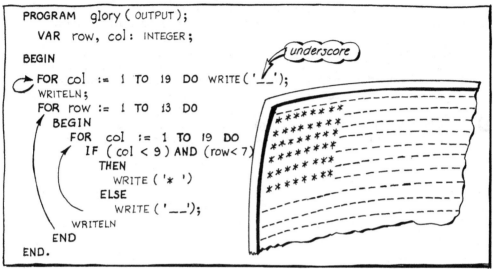

```pascal
PROGRAM   glory ( OUTPUT );

    VAR row, col: INTEGER;

BEGIN
    FOR col := 1 TO 19 DO WRITE ( '__' );
    WRITELN;
    FOR row := 1 TO 13 DO
      BEGIN
        FOR  col := 1 TO 19 DO
          IF ( col < 9 ) AND (row< 7)
            THEN
              WRITE ( '* ' )
            ELSE
              WRITE ( '__' );
        WRITELN
      END
END.
```

underscore

SINUOUS

A PROGRAM TO PLOT A SINUOUS CURVE USING A LOOP AND A VARIABLE FIELD WIDTH

The following program plots the graph of *sin(x)* scaled and offset from the left margin so that the curve oscillates about the middle of the screen. The trick of this kind of plot is to use an *expression* for field width. The field width varies from line to line; the asterisk is right-justified in each field.

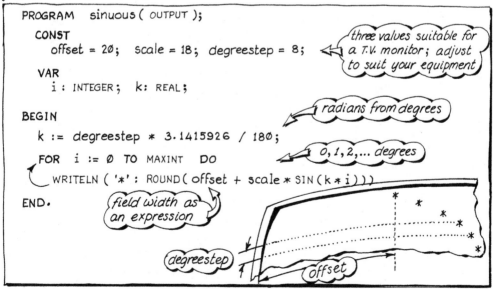

```pascal
PROGRAM   sinuous ( OUTPUT );

    CONST
      offset = 20;   scale = 18;   degreestep = 8;

    VAR
      i : INTEGER;   k: REAL;

BEGIN
    k := degreestep * 3.1415926 / 180;

    FOR  i := 0 TO MAXINT   DO
      WRITELN ( '*': ROUND( offset + scale * SIN ( k * i ) ) )
END.
```

three values suitable for a T.V. monitor; adjust to suit your equipment

radians from degrees

0, 1, 2,... degrees

field width as an expression

degreestep

offset

EXERCISES

1. Implement the *loans* program and experiment with different sets of data. If you enter zero for the percentage rate of interest the program fails. Include a test in the program for this eventuality and make the program print the results for it. If your Pascal permits interactive input make the program prompt its user for the three items of data required.

2. Implement the *shapes* program. Improve the program by making it return for a new problem having displayed a result. Let the program treat the letter Z as a stopping code (i.e. it should recognize R, T, C and Z).

3. Implement the *sinuous* program. Dampen the wave it produces by plotting $y = \sin x\ /\ \exp x$ instead of $y = \sin x$.

SYNTAX

Notice the different styles of writing in the introductory program; here it is again:

```
PROGRAM   painting( INPUT, OUTPUT);
   CONST    pi = 3.14;
   VAR      diameter, height, coverage, top,
            wall, pots: REAL;
BEGIN
   READ( diameter, height, coverage );
   top := pi * SQR( diameter )/ 4.0;
   wall := pi * diameter * height;
   pots := ( top + wall )/ coverage ;
   fullpots := TRUNC( pots ) + 1;
   WRITE('You need', fullpots, ' pots')
END .
```

When dealing with Pascal programs the computer makes no distinction between capital letters and corresponding lower-case letters except for those between apostrophes. So the program could be typed all in capitals:

```
PROGRAM  PAINTING( INPUT, OUTPUT);
   CONST PI = 3.14;
```

or all in lower-case letters:

```
   var diameter, height, coverage, top,
       wall, pots: real;
```

or in a mixture of capitals and lower-case letters:

```
   FullPots := TRUNC( Pots) + 1;
```

Only between one apostrophe and the next is case significant:

Write ('You need', FullPots, ' pots')
case not significant   *case is significant*   *case not significant*   *signif-icant*

But in the introductory example ⇆ and throughout the rest of this book ⇆ three styles of writing are employed so as to emphasize the three kinds of word in Pascal:

- PROGRAM, CONST, VAR, BEGIN,... are *reserved words* which behave like punctuation marks, each having a unique meaning in Pascal

- INPUT, REAL, READ, TRUNC,... are *predefined names*; they nominate facilities offered by Pascal for declaring files (⟨ INPUT ⟩), types (⟨ REAL ⟩) or invoking useful functions (⟨ WRITE( ), TRUNC( ) ⟩) but the programmer is free to ignore such facilities and use their names for other purposes

- painting, pi, diameter, height,... are names composed by the programmer to identify variables, constants, procedures and other things yet to be introduced.

It makes a program easier to understand when the kind of name or word is at once evident from the way it is written.

 **TO DESCRIBE THE WRITTEN FORM OF PASCAL'S DECLARATIONS AND STATEMENTS**

To define the written form and punctuation of Pascal programs it helps to use a concise notation. The notation described below is a blend of two notations in common use for defining the syntax of Pascal: railway-track diagrams, as used in several books on Pascal, and Backus-Naur Form (BNF) as used in the ISO definition of Pascal. Railway-track diagrams are visually confusing when following all but the simplest layouts; BNF is good for formal definitions but not so good for quick reference or general appraisal of a syntactical structure. The notation described below is intended for quick reference *and* general appraisal with little (if any) loss of rigour.

italics	Italic letters are used to name the entities being defined: *digit, operator, expression* and so on
::=	says " is defined to be ... " as in BNF
ROMANS, & + (* / ˉ 012 etc.	These stand for themselves; copy them from the definitions just as they are. Substitute lower-case letters if preferred: a for A, b for B, c for C etc.

Vertical bars enclosing several rows offer a choice of precisely one row

This arrow says the item(s) over which it is drawn are optional (may be skipped over)

This arrow permits return ⇌ hence offers the choice of another item from vertical bars or the same item as before

A circle (or sausage shape) contains the separator to use when returning for another item. No circle means no separator.

*name*_{var}
const
file
type
fn
proc

A subscript to *name* tells what that name is naming; whether a *variable*, a *constant*, a *file*, a *type*, a *function*, a *procedure*. (This device goes beyond syntax into the domain of semantics.)

▶   This symbol is put in front of illustrations in place of the words " for example "

Several words used in the definitions below are different from those in standard works on Pascal. In particular, I use *name* in place of *identifier*, *term* in place of *factor*, and have no need of a word in place of *term*. I use *comparator* in place of *relational operator*.

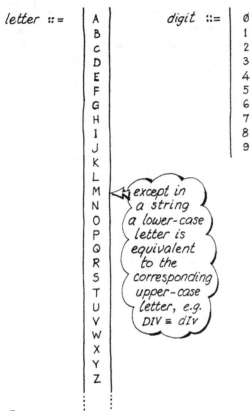

letter ::=
A B C D E F G H I J K L M N O P Q R S T U V W X Y Z

except in a string a lower-case letter is equivalent to the corresponding upper-case letter, e.g. DIV ≡ dIv

digit ::=
0 1 2 3 4 5 6 7 8 9

symbol ::=
+ − * / = < > [ ] . , ? : ; ↑ ( )

Also the lower-case letters if available.

Notice that apostrophe and braces {'} do not appear in the definition of *symbol*; they are dealt with explicitly.

Other symbols such as £ and ! and $ (as available) may be used in a *string* or *comment*.

space ::= *space bar pressed once*

Spaces are significant in strings and comments. New lines are not permitted in strings or comments.

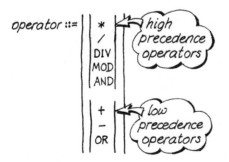

operator ::=
* / DIV MOD AND *high precedence operators*

+ − OR *low precedence operators*

comparator ::=
lower precedence than that of any operator

< <= = > >= <> IN

In the expression 3+4*5 the * is applied before + because it is of higher precedence. Use brackets to override: e.g. (3+4)*5

The expression 5−3 = 2 is *true* because it is treated as (5−3)=2, not as 5−(3=2). In other words the comparator has lower precedence.

24

COMPOUNDS

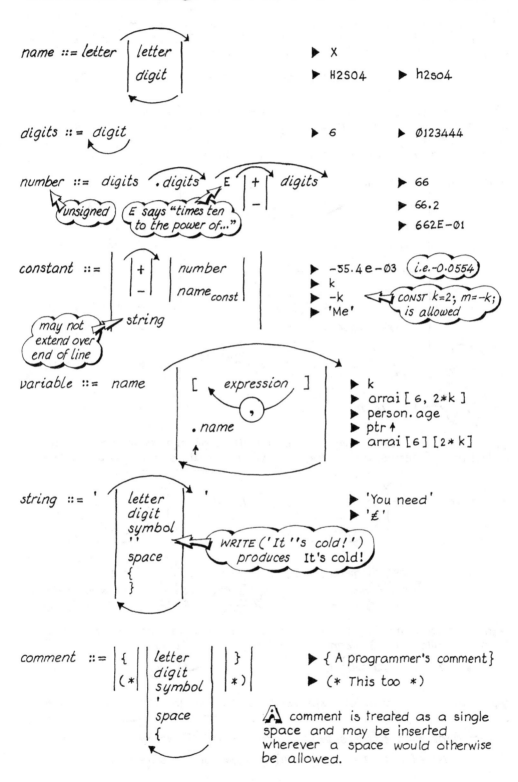

name ::= letter | letter / digit

▶ X

▶ H2SO4   ▶ h2so4

digits ::= digit

▶ 6   ▶ Ø123444

number ::= digits . digits E + / − digits

unsigned   *E says "times ten to the power of..."*

▶ 66
▶ 66.2
▶ 662E−Ø1

constant ::= + / − | number / name_const

may not extend over end of line → string

▶ −55.4e−Ø3 (*i.e. −0.0554*)
▶ k
▶ −k ← *CONST k=2; m=−k; is allowed*
▶ 'Me'

variable ::= name [expression ,] . name ↑

▶ k
▶ arrai[6, 2*k]
▶ person.age
▶ ptr ↑
▶ arrai[6][2*k]

string ::= ' letter / digit / symbol / '' / space / { / } '

▶ 'You need'
▶ '£'

WRITE('It''s cold!') produces It's cold!

comment ::= { / (* letter / digit / symbol / ' / space / { } / *)

▶ { A programmer's comment}
▶ (* This too *)

A comment is treated as a single space and may be inserted wherever a space would otherwise be allowed.

SYNTAX OF AN EXPRESSION
& BOOLEAN EXPRESSION, ALSO CALLED A CONDITION

The "elements" and "compounds" of Pascal's syntax may now be combined in the definition of an *expression*. The introductory example shows several expressions of which the following two are typical:

$$(\text{top} + \text{wall}) / \text{coverage} ; \quad \text{pi} * \text{SQR} (\text{diameter}) / 4.0;$$

An *expression* comprises one or more *terms*. The terms are bound together with brackets and operators. A term may be the name of a variable ((e.g. top)) or a reference to a function ((e.g. TRUNC(pots))) or one of several other forms defined below.

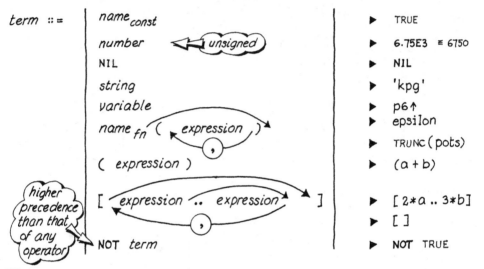

term ::=	
name_{const}	▶ TRUE
number ⟵ unsigned	▶ 6.75E3 ≡ 6750
NIL	▶ NIL
string	▶ 'kpg'
variable	▶ p6↑
name_{fn} (expression ,)	▶ epsilon
	▶ TRUNC (pots)
(expression)	▶ (a + b)
[expression .. expression ,]	▶ [2*a .. 3*b]
	▶ [ ]
(higher precedence than that of any operator) NOT term	▶ **NOT** TRUE

Having defined *term*, here is the definition of *expression* which is a collection of terms bound together with operators and comparators :

$$\text{expression} ::= \left|\begin{matrix}+\\-\end{matrix}\right| \to \text{term} \circlearrowleft (\text{operator}) \quad \text{comparator} \left|\begin{matrix}+\\-\end{matrix}\right| \to \text{term} \circlearrowleft (\text{operator})$$

▶ (pi * SQR(diameter) / 4) + (pi * diameter * height)
both high precedence *low precedence* *(brackets not necessary in this example because of precedence)*

An expression involving one or more comparators, or a single Boolean term, is called a *Boolean expression* or *condition*.

▶ −3 > 1 ⟵ *false*   ▶ TRUE ⟵ *true*

An exceptional form of expression is allowed in WRITE and WRITELN statements :

exceptional ::= expression ⌢ : expression ⌢ : expression

▶ WRITE (x : 8 : 2)   ▶ WRITELN('*' : ROUND (offset + scale *SIN(k*i)))

SOME FORMS HAVE NOT
YET BEEN INTRODUCED

The definition of *statement* is set out below. Several of these forms of *statement* have not yet been introduced.

null statement

$statement ::= digits :$

label for GOTO

$variable := expression$ ← *assignment*

$name_{fn} := expression$

$name_{proc}$ (| $expression$ |)

$name_{fn}$ ← *function-names as parameters*

,

BEGIN $statement$ END   *compound statement*

;

IF $condition$ THEN $statement$ ELSE $statement$

REPEAT $statement$ UNTIL $condition$

;

WHILE $condition$ DO $statement$

FOR $name_{var} := expression$ | TO | $expression$ DO $statement$
| DOWNTO |

CASE $expression$ OF $constant$: $statement$; END

,

;

WITH $variable$ DO $statement$

,

GOTO $digits$

▶ 100 : area := pi * SQR(diameter) / 4 ← *assignment statement ⇌ labelled*

▶ BEGIN temp := a; a := b; b := temp END ← *compound statement*

▶ IF a > b THEN BEGIN temp := a; a := b; b := temp END ← *IF statement*

▶ BEGIN ; t := a; ; a := b; b := t; END

null statements

27

Here is a "top-down" definition of *program* :

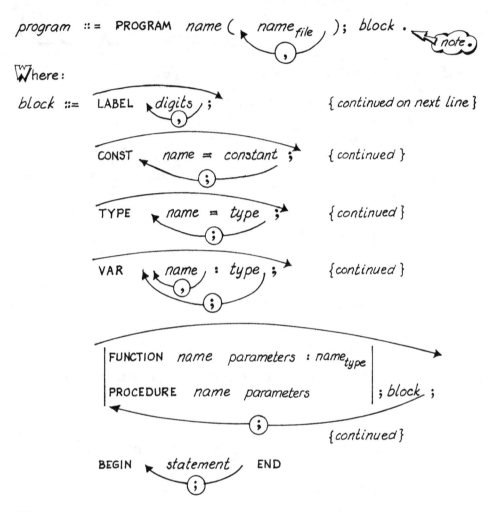

program ::= PROGRAM *name* (*name*$_{file}$,); *block* . *note.*

Where:

block ::= LABEL *digits* ; ,   { continued on next line }

     CONST *name* = *constant* ; ;   { continued }

     TYPE *name* = *type* ; ;   { continued }

     VAR *name* , : *type* ; ;   { continued }

     FUNCTION *name* *parameters* : *name*$_{type}$

     PROCEDURE *name* *parameters*   ; *block* ; ;

                 { continued }

     BEGIN *statement* ; END

Where:

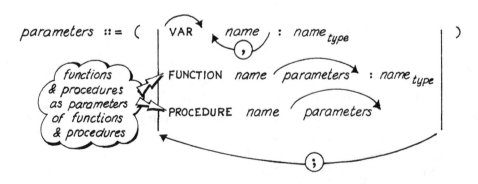

parameters ::= (VAR *name* , : *name*$_{type}$)

functions & procedures as parameters of functions & procedures

FUNCTION *name* *parameters* : *name*$_{type}$

PROCEDURE *name* *parameters* ;

SYNTAX OF TYPE

Here is a top-down definition of *type*:

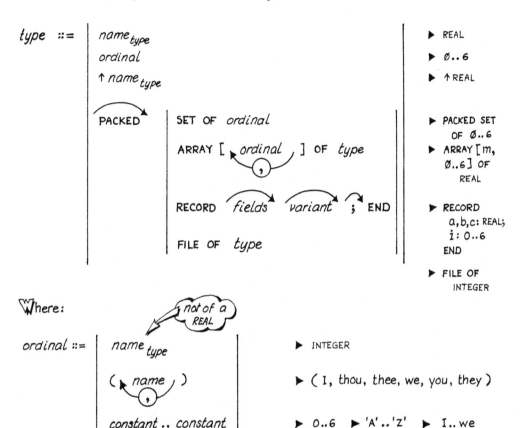

type ::=
| name*type*
| ordinal
| ↑ name*type*

PACKED →
SET OF *ordinal*
ARRAY [*ordinal* ,] OF *type*
RECORD *fields* *variant* ; END
FILE OF *type*

▶ REAL
▶ Ø..6
▶ ↑ REAL
▶ PACKED SET OF Ø..6
▶ ARRAY [m, Ø..6] OF REAL
▶ RECORD a, b, c: REAL; i: 0..6 END
▶ FILE OF INTEGER

Where:

ordinal ::=
| name *type* (*not of a REAL*)
| (name ,)
| constant .. constant

▶ INTEGER
▶ (I, thou, thee, we, you, they)
▶ 0..6   ▶ 'A'..'z'   ▶ I.. we

And where:

fields ::= name , : type ;

▶ nr, age: INTEGER; status: CHAR

And where:

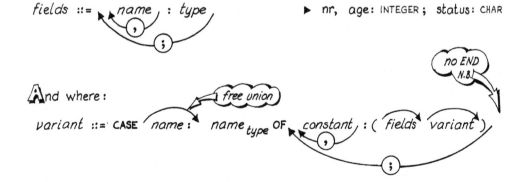

variant ::= CASE *name* : name *type* OF *constant* , : (*fields* *variant*) ; (*free union*) (*no END N.B.!*)

That completes the definition of the syntax of ISO Pascal.

ARITHMETIC

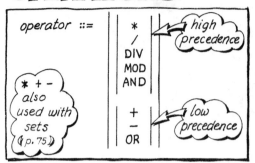
OPERATORS

```
operator ::=        *          ╭ high ╮
                    /          │ precedence │
                    DIV        ╰──────╯
                    MOD
                    AND
* + -
also                +          ╭ low ╮
used with           -          │ precedence │
sets                OR         ╰──────╯
(p.75)
```

The syntax of *operator* is defined again here for convenience.

The use of these operators is explained on this double page. The syntax of *expression* on page 26 should be consulted if the use of brackets in these examples is not immediately clear.

In the absence of brackets an expression is evaluated from left to right, applying high precedence operators before low precedence operators. Brackets may be included to enforce any desired order of evaluation. For example a * b / c and (a * b)/c would be evaluated in the same way but a * (b/c) would enforce a change in the order of operations.

The operators DIV and MOD are for integer division; they yield an integer quotient and remainder respectively:

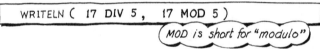

```
WRITELN ( 17 DIV 5 , 17 MOD 5 )
```
MOD is short for "modulo"

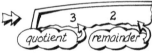

```
    3       2
quotient  remainder
```

For positive values of i and j the following relationship holds:

$$(i \ DIV \ j) * j + (i \ MOD \ j) = i$$

```
WRITELN ( ( 17 DIV 5 ) * 5 + ( 17 MOD 5 ) )
```

```
        17
```

But complications arise with non-positive values. The second operand of MOD is not allowed to be negative:

```
WRITELN ( 17 MOD −5     )
```

```
Error
```

Permissible arrangements are permuted below:

```
WRITELN ( 17 DIV 5,     17 MOD 5 );
WRITELN ( 17 DIV (−5));
WRITELN (−17 DIV 5,    −17 MOD 5 );
WRITELN (−17 DIV (−5))
```

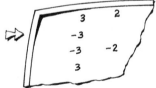

```
    3       2
   −3
   −3      −2
    3
```

and when the first operand is smaller in absolute value:

```
WRITELN ( 5 DIV 17,     5 MOD 17 );
WRITELN ( 5 DIV (−17));
WRITELN (−5 DIV 17,    −5 MOD 17 );
WRITELN (−5 DIV (−17) )
```

```
    0       5
    0
    0      −5
    0
```

An error is reported if a divisor is zero, or either operand not an integer:

```
WRITELN ( 17 DIV 0     );
WRITELN ( 17.0    MOD 5 )
```

```
Error
Error
```

The operators + and − may be used as "monadic" operators ⟨ in other words as signs ⟩ in front of integer or real expressions:

```
WRITELN ( −2, +2 * 3 );
WRITELN ( −2.0: 4: 1 )
```

⇒

```
        −2      6
  −2.0
```

The operators * and + and − produce an integer result when *both* operands represent integers:

```
WRITELN ( 2*3,  2+3,  2−3 )
```

⇒

```
     6   5   −1
```

but produce a real result if either or both operands represent a real:

```
WRITELN ( 2.0*3: 4: 1 );
WRITELN ( 2 + 3.0: 4: 1 )
```

⇒

```
  6.0
  5.0
```

The operator / produces a real result ≋ even when both operands represent integers:

```
WRITELN ( 6/2   :4 : 1 );
WRITELN ( 6.0/2 :4 : 1 )
```

⇒

```
  3.0
  3.0
```

The divisor is not allowed to represent zero:

```
WRITELN ( 6/0    :4  :1 )
```

⇒

```
Error
```

The operators **AND** and **OR** between Boolean operands produce a Boolean result. Errors are reported if the operands are not Boolean:

```
WRITELN ( 1 OR    2 );
WRITELN ( 'A' AND    'B' )
```

only comparators may be used with type CHAR e.g. 'A' < 'B'

⇒

```
Error
Error
```

The following *truth tables* define the Boolean results obtained when applying AND and OR operators to Boolean operands:

AND	SECOND OPERAND	
FIRST OPERAND	true	false
true	✓	✗
false	✗	✗

OR	SECOND OPERAND	
FIRST OPERAND	true	false
true	✓	✓
false	✓	✗

Here are some examples of Boolean expressions. Notice how the WRITELN statement produces Boolean results as words. Whether these words emerge in capitals or lower-case letters depends on the installation:

```
WRITELN ( TRUE  AND TRUE,   TRUE   AND  FALSE );
WRITELN ( FALSE  AND TRUE,   FALSE  AND  FALSE );
WRITELN ( TRUE  OR TRUE,   TRUE  OR   FALSE );
WRITELN ( FALSE  OR TRUE,   FALSE  OR   FALSE );
WRITELN ( (((1=2) OR (1+2=3)) OR (1>2)) AND (2+3=5))
```

⇒

```
  true      false
  false     false
  true      true
  true      false
  true
```

SIZE AND PRECISION

An integer may be positive or zero or negative. A copy of the biggest allowable integer that can be handed or stored is held as a constant named MAXINT:

MAXINT 32767

value differs from one installation to another; find out what it is on yours by running this little program

```
PROGRAM findout (OUTPUT);
BEGIN
   WRITE ( MAXINT )
END.
```

The value 32767 is usual for installations in which integers are stored as 16-bit words. A value of 2147483647 is usual where 32-bit words are employed.

If the program tries to evaluate an integer expression for which an intermediate result grows bigger than MAXINT an error message is evoked. It may be possible to avoid this by adding brackets to an expression; for instance changing i * j DIV k   to   i * (j DIV k).

Although the allowable range of integer is −MAXINT to +MAXINT you may discover that a value of −(MAXINT +1) causes no error. This is because a commonly used range of integers stored in n-bit words runs from -2^{n-1} to $(2^{n-1}-1)$ (asymmetrical about zero).

A real number may be negative, zero or positive. Its maximum absolute value is 10^{38}; a typical precision is 6 to 7 significant decimal digits. On such an installation the biggest positive or negative number would be about:

± 100, 000, 000, 000, 000, 000, 000, 000, 000, 000, 000, 000

The smallest positive or negative number would be about:

± 0. 000, 000, 000, 000, 000, 000, 000, 000, 000, 000, 000, 000, 01

The number 1,000,000 would be just distinguishable (with the above precision) from 1,000,001 but not from 1,000,000.1 .

Numbers are stored as binary digits (bits) rather than decimal digits, hence the unavoidable vagueness of the above two paragraphs. The range of real numbers is depicted below :

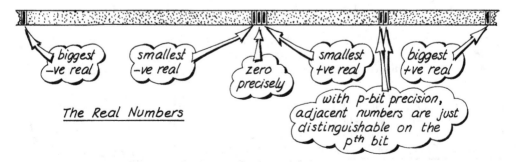

biggest −ve real • smallest −ve real • zero precisely • smallest +ve real • biggest +ve real

with p-bit precision, adjacent numbers are just distinguishable on the pth bit

The Real Numbers

COMPARATORS

((OFFICIALLY "RELATIONAL OPERATORS"))
BOOLEAN RESULT FROM COMPATIBLE OPERANDS

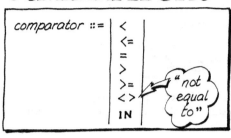

```
comparator ::=   <
                 <=
                 =
                 >
                 >=         "not
                 <>         equal
                 IN          to"
```

The syntax of *comparator* is reproduced here for convenience. The symbols have the conventional significance; >= for example says "Greater than or equal to".

The precedence of any *comparator* is lower than that of any *operator*.

The syntax of *expression* is also reproduced so as to emphasize the difference in usage between *operator* and *comparator*:

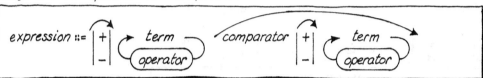

Terms of like type may be compared, the result being a Boolean value:

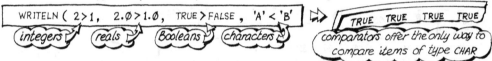

WRITELN (2>1, 2.0>1.0, TRUE>FALSE, 'A' < 'B') ⇒ TRUE TRUE TRUE TRUE

integers *reals* *Booleans* *characters*

comparators offer the only way to compare items of type CHAR

Real and integer terms of like value are interchangeable:

WRITELN (2 > 1.0,   2.0 > 1) *types mixed* ⇒ TRUE TRUE

The syntax diagram for *expression* allows only one comparator. But *expression in brackets* is a form of *term*, so a further comparator may then be included to make a more complicated expression thus:

term ⇒ 2 > 1 ⇐ *term* — *an expression*
term ⇒ (2 > 1) = (3 > 2) ⇐ *term* — *a more complicated expression*
comparator

Sets are explained in chapter 7, but the following operations on sets are reproduced below for completeness. The names "friends" and "acquaintances" are names of sets; "ffoulkes" is the name of a single member of a set.

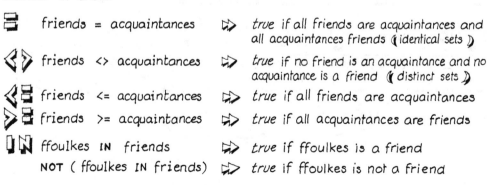

friends = acquaintances ⇒ *true if all friends are acquaintances and all acquaintances friends ((identical sets))*

friends <> acquaintances ⇒ *true if no friend is an acquaintance and no acquaintance is a friend ((distinct sets))*

friends <= acquaintances ⇒ *true if all friends are acquaintances*

friends >= acquaintances ⇒ *true if all acquaintances are friends*

ffoulkes IN friends ⇒ *true if ffoulkes is a friend*

NOT (ffoulkes IN friends) ⇒ *true if ffoulkes is not a friend*

ARITHMETIC FUNCTIONS

For years functions have enjoyed *arguments*:

$$x := ABS (y)$$

function — *argument* — PARAMETER!

but the preferred terminology for *argument* in Pascal is *parameter*. The parameters described below are *actual* parameters. Later we define *formal* parameters hitherto known as *dummy arguments*.

The following two functions may be given an integer parameter, in which case they return an integer result. These functions may be given a real parameter, in which case they return a real result.

ABS (*expression*)
THE ABSOLUTE (i.e. POSITIVE) VALUE
OF ITS PARAMETER

```
WRITELN( ABS(-2), ABS(0), ABS(2) );
WRITELN ( ABS (-2.0):4:1, ABS(0.0):4:1, ABS(2.0):4:1 )
```
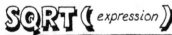

```
            2      0      2
         2.0   0.0   2.0
```

SQR (*expression*)
THE SQUARE OF THE VALUE
OF ITS PARAMETER

```
WRITELN (SQR(-2), SQR(0), SQR(2) );
WRITELN (SQR(-2.0):4:1, SQR(0.0):4:1, SQR(2.0):4:1 )
```

```
            4      0      4
         4.0   0.0   4.0
```

The remaining arithmetical functions may be given an integer or real parameter, but return a real value in either case:

SQRT (*expression*)
THE SQUARE ROOT OF ITS PARAMETER
WHICH MUST NOT BE NEGATIVE

```
WRITELN ( SQRT (16):4:1, SQRT(0.64):4:1, SQRT(0):4:1 );
WRITELN ( SQRT (-16)) .
```

```
         4.0  0.8   0.0
      Error
```

LN (*expression*)
THE NATURAL LOGARITHM (BASE e) OF ITS
PARAMETER WHICH MUST BE POSITIVE

```
WRITELN (LN(1):4:1, LN(2.718282):4:1, LN(7.5):4:1 );
WRITELN (LN(0),        LN(-1) )
```

```
         0.0  1.0  2.0
      Error
```

EXP (*expression*)
THE NATURAL ANTILOGARITHM (BASE e).
IN OTHER WORDS EXP(x) SIGNIFIES e^x

```
WRITELN (EXP(0):4:1, EXP(1):8:5, EXP(2.014903):4:1);
WRITELN (EXP(-1):7:4,    EXP(LN (100):6:1 )
```

```
         1.0  2.71828   7.5
      0.3679  100.0
```

$e^{-1} \equiv \frac{1}{e}$

$e = 1 + \frac{1}{1!} + \frac{1}{2!} + \frac{1}{3!} + \dots$

TRIGONOMETRICAL FUNCTIONS

The trigonometrical functions are defined below; each may be given an integer or real parameter but returns a real result in either case.

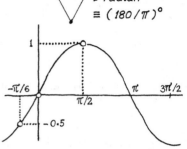

1 radian $\equiv (180/\pi)^\circ$

SIN (expression)

THE SINE OF AN ANGLE MEASURED IN RADIANS

$$\sin \alpha = \frac{p}{h}$$

CONST   PI = 3.1415926;

```
WRITELN ( SIN(-PI/6):4:1);
WRITELN ( SIN(∅):4:1);
WRITELN ( SIN(PI/2):4:1)
```

```
-0.5
 0.0
 1.0
```

COS (expression)

THE COSINE OF AN ANGLE MEASURED IN RADIANS

$$\cos \alpha = \frac{a}{h}$$

CONST   PI = 3.1415926;

```
WRITELN ( COS(-PI/6):8:5);
WRITELN ( COS(∅):4:1);
WRITELN ( COS(PI):4:1)
```

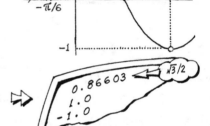

```
0.86603     √3/2
1.0
-1.0
```

ARCTAN (expression)

THE ARCTANGENT { "THE ANGLE, IN RADIANS, WHOSE TANGENT IS ..." }

$$\arctan(p/a) = \alpha \text{ radians}$$

effectively infinite

```
WRITELN ( ARCTAN(1E35):8:5 );
WRITELN ( ARCTAN(∅):4:1);
WRITELN ( ARCTAN(-1):8:5)
```

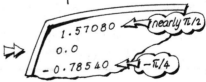

```
1.57080     nearly π/2
0.0
-0.78540    -π/4
```

TRANSFER FUNCTIONS

When an integer result is assigned to a real variable the result is automatically converted to type real, no function being needed. This facility is called *implicit type conversion*.

```
VAR x,y: REAL;  i,j: INTEGER;
```

```
x := 2*3+4;  ← converted from
                10 to 10.0
y := 3       ← converted to 3.0
```

There is no converse of the above; it is wrong to assign a real result to an integer variable.

```
i := 2.0 *3 + 4;
j := 9/3
```

A real value must either be *truncated* or *rounded* before being assigned to an integer variable, the functions TRUNC( ) and ROUND( ) being provided for the purpose.

real

TRUNC (*expression*)

TRUNCATE ANY FRACTIONAL PART OF THE REAL VALUE AND CONVERT TO TYPE INTEGER

```
WRITELN ( TRUNC (3.1),   TRUNC (3.8) );

WRITELN ( TRUNC (-3.1),  TRUNC (-3.8) );

WRITELN ( TRUNC (3.0),   TRUNC (-3.0))
```

⟹

```
     3        3
    -3       -3
     3       -3
```

real

ROUND (*expression*)

ROUND TO NEAREST WHOLE NUMBER AND CONVERT TO TYPE INTEGER

```
WRITELN ( ROUND (3.1),    ROUND (3.8) );

WRITELN ( ROUND (-3.1),   ROUND (-3.8) );

WRITELN ( ROUND (3.0),    ROUND (-3.0) );

WRITELN ( ROUND (3.5),    ROUND (-3.5))
```

⟹

```
     3        4
    -3       -4
     3       -3
     4       -4
```

There can be surprises. Consider a value of 3.499999 stored in a real variable x. If this value were displayed using the statement WRITE (x: 8: 5) it would appear as 3.50000, but WRITE(ROUND(x)) would yield 3 rather than 4. This problem may be avoided by a "nudge" such as WRITE (ROUND (x + 0.000001)) (assuming the value stored in variable x is known to be positive).

It is wrong to give an integer parameter to TRUNC( ) or ROUND( ).

```
WRITELN ( TRUNC (3) );

WRITELN ( ROUND (3) )
```

⟹

```
Error
Error
```

BOOLEAN FUNCTIONS

RETURNING TRUE or FALSE
ODD( ), EOLN( ), EOF( )

The function ODD( ) is for revealing whether the result of an integer expression is odd or even.

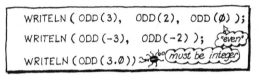 (*expression*)

RETURNS TRUE IF PARAMETER REDUCES TO AN ODD INTEGER ~ OTHERWISE RETURNS FALSE

```
WRITELN ( ODD(3),  ODD(2),  ODD(∅) );
WRITELN ( ODD(-3),  ODD(-2) );   "even"
WRITELN ( ODD( 3.0))   must be integer
```

```
TRUE FALSE FALSE
TRUE FALSE
Error
```

The following functions are for detecting the end of a line and the end of a file respectively. EOLN is usable only with *text* files which are organized as lines of items. Files are described in chapter 10; below is enough information to explain the use of EOLN in the early examples. Do not use EOF if data come from the keyboard; chapter 11 deals with this precaution.

EOLN (*name_file*) RETURNS TRUE IF THE FINAL ITEM OF THE CURRENT LINE HAS BEEN READ

EOLN ← implies EOLN(INPUT)

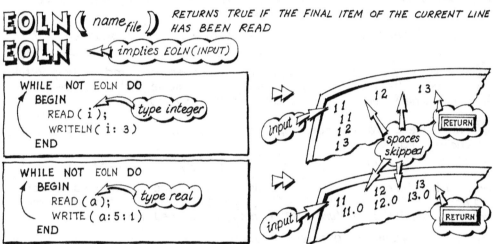

EOF (*name_file*) RETURNS TRUE IF THE FINAL ITEM ON THE FILE HAS BEEN READ (OBEYING ANOTHER READ WOULD CAUSE FAILURE)

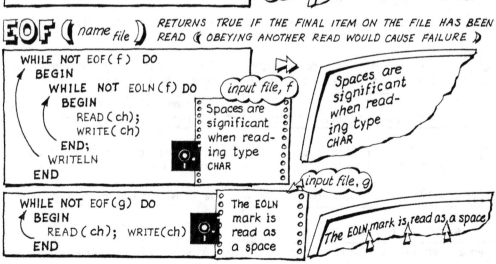

ORDINAL FUNCTIONS

The letters 'A' to 'Z' run in *ascending order*; in other words each letter has an *ordinal value* to establish its relative order in the alphabet. This ordinal value may be obtained from the ORD( ) function:

ORD(*expression* **)** RETURNS THE ORDINAL VALUE OF THE CHARACTER ≈ OR OTHER ORDERED TYPE ≈ EXPRESSED BY THE PARAMETER

WRITELN (ORD ('I'), ORD('J'))	⇨	73 74	201 209
		ASCII code	EBCDIC code

The ordinal value of a character depends on the computer installation, the ASCII code being typical on personal and home computers. But whatever the code employed the ordinal values of letters run in ascending order:

$$ORD('A') < ORD('B') < ORD('c')... < ORD('z')$$

but ORD('z') − ORD('A') is *not* necessarily 25. Not all computers offer the lower-case letters, but for those that do:

$$ORD('a') < ORD('b') < ORD('c')... < ORD('z')$$

There is no *defined* relationship between upper-case and corresponding lower-case letters but it should be safe to assume that ORD('a')−ORD('A') has the same value through the alphabet to ORD('z')−ORD('Z').

Whatever the character code employed, the ordinal values of *digits* run in ascending order:

$$ORD('0') < ORD('1') < ORD('2')... < ORD('9')$$

and furthermore there is a difference of 1 between ordinal values of adjacent digits, so ORD('9')−ORD('0') = 9. It follows that the numerical value of digit *d* (*type CHAR*) may be obtained from:

$$value := ORD(d) - ORD('0')$$

(There is probably *no* Pascal installation at which ORD('0') returns zero.)

Types CHAR, INTEGER *etc.* are provided by Pascal, but the programmer may define other types by *enumerating* a sequence of constants:

TYPE	
days = (mon, tue, wed, thu, fri, sat, sun);	*enumerated types are explained on page 72*

Constants of enumerated type have ordinal values counted from zero. For example ORD(mon) returns 0, ORD(sun) returns 6; mon < sun.

Type BOOLEAN is an enumerated type which is provided automatically as:

TYPE
BOOLEAN = (FALSE, TRUE);

hence ORD(FALSE) returns 0, ORD(TRUE) returns 1; FALSE < TRUE

The converse of ORD( ) is CHR( ):

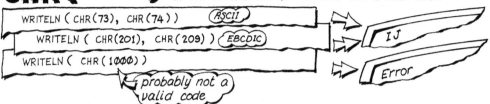

CHR(*expression* **)** RETURNS THE CHARACTER WHOSE ORDINAL VALUE IS EXPRESSED BY ITS PARAMETER ↦ ERROR IF NOT A VALID CODE

```
WRITELN ( CHR(73), CHR(74) )          (ASCII)
WRITELN ( CHR(201), CHR(209) )  (EBCDIC)          ⇨   I J
WRITELN ( CHR(1000) )                              ⇨   Error
```
← probably not a valid code

If something has an ordinal value it is seldom necessary to know what that value actually is; it is enough to ask for the successor or predecessor in the established order. Functions SUCC( ) and PRED( ) are provided for this purpose:

SUCC(*expression* **)** RETURNS THE SUCCESSOR TO THE ITEM EXPRESSED BY THE PARAMETER

```
WRITELN ( SUCC ('A'), SUCC ('Ø'), SUCC(0) );
WRITELN ( SUCC (FALSE) );
WRITELN ( SUCC ('z') )  →  'z' has no successor
```
⇨
```
B 1          1
TRUE
Error
```

PRED(*expression* **)** RETURNS THE PREDECESSOR TO THE ITEM EXPRESSED BY THE PARAMETER

```
WRITELN ( PRED ('z'), PRED('9'), PRED(9) );
WRITELN ( PRED (TRUE) );
WRITELN ( PRED ('A') )  →  'A' has no predecessor
```
⇨
```
Y 8          8
FALSE
Error
```

These two functions may be used to obtain successors and predecessors of enumerated types. Referring to type *days* defined opposite:

PRED(sun) *returns* sat,   SUCC(mon) *returns* tue

but it would be wrong to illustrate this as WRITELN (PRED (sun)) because enumerated types cannot be read or written ↝ a constraint on their usefulness. The nearest thing to WRITELN (PRED (sun)) is WRITELN (ORD (PRED (sun))) which would cause 5 to be written (the ordinal value of sat).

The SUCC( ) function is handy for controlling loops:

```
i := Ø;
REPEAT
   i := SUCC ( i );

   statements

UNTIL  i = 1Ø
```

41

5

CONTROL

FLOW CHARTS
IF • *THEN* • *ELSE* STATEMENT
FOR LOOP
REPEAT LOOP
WHILE LOOP
FILTER (EXAMPLE)
CASE STATEMENT
SYMBOL-STATE TABLE (EXAMPLE)

FLOW CHARTS

Most of the control statements have been introduced by example in earlier chapters; in this chapter they are defined and their characteristics explained. Unless disturbed by one of these statements, control goes from statement to statement sequentially.

The behaviour of each control statement is depicted on this double page as a flow chart.

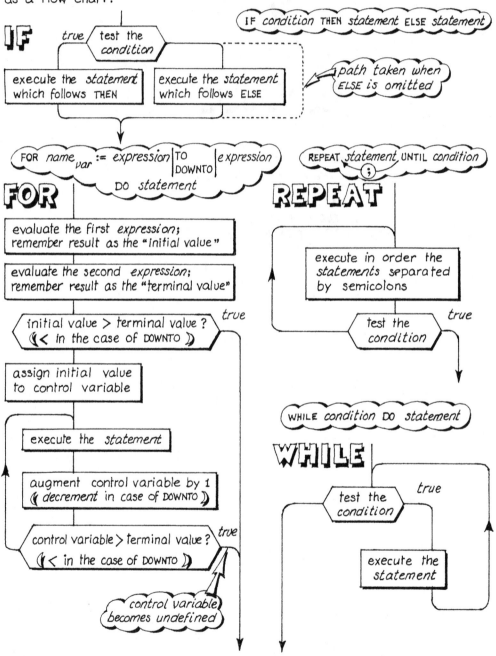

IF *condition* THEN *statement* ELSE *statement*

IF — true / test the condition

execute the *statement* which follows THEN

execute the *statement* which follows ELSE

path taken when ELSE is omitted

FOR *name*~var~ := *expression* | TO DOWNTO | *expression* DO *statement*

FOR

evaluate the first *expression*; remember result as the "initial value"

evaluate the second *expression*; remember result as the "terminal value"

initial value > terminal value ? (< in the case of DOWNTO) true

assign initial value to control variable

execute the *statement*

augment control variable by 1 (*decrement* in case of DOWNTO)

control variable > terminal value ? (< in the case of DOWNTO) true

control variable becomes undefined

REPEAT *statement* ; UNTIL *condition*

REPEAT

execute in order the statements separated by semicolons

test the condition true

WHILE *condition* DO *statement*

WHILE

test the condition true

execute the statement

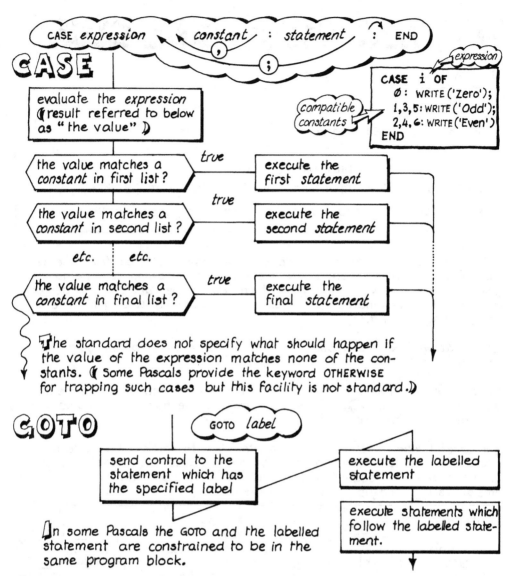

CASE

CASE *expression* , *constant* : *statement* ; END

evaluate the *expression* (result referred to below as "the value")

compatible constants

```
CASE i OF
  Ø: WRITE('Zero');
  1,3,5: WRITE('Odd');
  2,4,6: WRITE('Even')
END
```
← *expression*

the value matches a *constant* in first list? — *true* → execute the first *statement*

the value matches a *constant* in second list? — *true* → execute the second *statement*

etc.   etc.

the value matches a *constant* in final list? — *true* → execute the final *statement*

The standard does not specify what should happen if the value of the expression matches none of the constants. (Some Pascals provide the keyword OTHERWISE for trapping such cases but this facility is not standard.)

GOTO

GOTO *label*

send control to the statement which has the specified label

execute the labelled statement

execute statements which follow the labelled statement.

In some Pascals the GOTO and the labelled statement are constrained to be in the same program block.

The GOTO is useful for error recovery in interactive systems ≈ a subject beyond the scope of this book.

EXIT?   PASCAL LACKS AN EXIT STATEMENT

Standard Pascal offers no way to jump out of the middle of a loop[†]. But here is a contrivance:

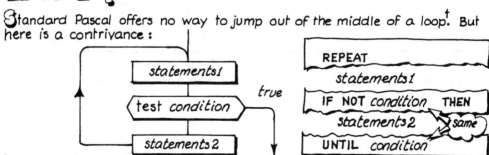

statements1

test condition — *true*

statements2

```
REPEAT
  statements1
  IF NOT condition THEN
    statements2
UNTIL condition
```
same

[†] apart from GOTO

IF ~ THEN ~ ELSE STATEMENT

The syntax of the IF statement is:

> IF *condition* THEN *statement* ⌢ ELSE *statement*
>
> ▶ IF profit > loss THEN WRITE ('Hooray!')
> ▶ IF profit > loss THEN WRITE ('Hooray!') ELSE WRITE ('Bother')
> ▶ IF initial > 'K' AND initial < 'S' THEN WRITE ('See L to R directory')

When *condition* is evaluated, and its value turns out to be *true*, the statement following THEN is obeyed ⇌ the statement following ELSE being ignored. Conversely, if the value turns out to be *false*, the statement following THEN is ignored ⇌ the statement following ELSE ❨ if there is one ❩ being obeyed.

If *condition* does not reduce to *true* or *false* an error message is evoked.

The *statement* following THEN or ELSE may be a compound statement ❨ *i.e.* BEGIN... ...END ❩. There is no limit to the number or complexity of statements comprising a compound statement.

Be careful when nesting IF statements. Try to employ the pattern "ELSE IF" rather than "THEN IF" which leaves an "ELSE" dangling in the brain. A sequence of "THEN IF" can conclude in an embarrassing pile-up of ELSE clauses:

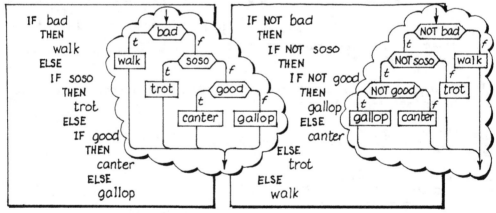

```
IF  bad                          IF NOT bad
    THEN                             THEN
        walk                             IF NOT soso
    ELSE                                     THEN
        IF soso                                  IF NOT good
            THEN                                     THEN
                trot                                     gallop
            ELSE                                 ELSE
                IF good                              canter
                    THEN                         ELSE
                        canter                       trot
                    ELSE                     ELSE
                        gallop                   walk
```

In general, ELSE refers to the closest preceding IF which has not yet been paired with an ELSE.

46

FOR LOOP

The syntax of the FOR statement is:

```
FOR name := expression | TO     | expression DO statement
                        | DOWNTO |
```
names the
control variable

▶ FOR humbug := 1 TO 3 DO WRITELN ('We wish you a merry Christmas');
  WRITELN ('And a happy new year')

▶ FOR m := 12 DOWNTO 2 DO WRITELN (m:3, ' men');
  WRITELN ('1 man & his dog went to mow a meadow')

The control variable may be any ordered type (typically INTEGER, never REAL). Both *expressions* must reduce to the same type of value as that of the control variable.

The flow chart on page 44 should be consulted on the patterns of behaviour illustrated below.

The two expressions are evaluated before any statement of the loop; they are not subsequently re-evaluated. If these expressions define an impossible sequence the loop is not executed at all:

```
FOR i := 2 TO 1 DO  WRITE ('Shy')
```
nothing written ≈ no error reported

It is impossible to "run away with the finishing line" which is frozen on entry:

```
finish := 3;
FOR i := 1 TO finish DO
BEGIN
    finish := finish + 1;
    WRITELN ( finish)
END
```
terminal value frozen at 3

precisely three times round

```
4
5
6
```

It is wrong to tamper with the control variable. Obvious cases of tampering involve assignment to the control variable and reading values into it:

```
FOR i := 1 TO 3 DO
BEGIN
    i := i - 1;
    READ (i);
    FOR i := 1 TO 3 DO WRITE ( 'Dear me!')
END
```

It is wrong to assume anything about the value in the control variable on emergence from a FOR loop (unless vacated by GOTO):

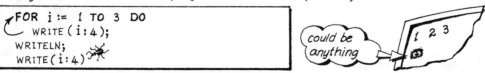

```
FOR i := 1 TO 3 DO
    WRITE ( i:4);
WRITELN;
WRITE (i:4)
```
could be anything

```
 1   2   3
```

REPEAT LOOP

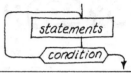

The syntax of the REPEAT statement is:

```
REPEAT  statement,  UNTIL  condition
            (;)

▶ n:=3;  REPEAT  n:= PRED(n); WRITELN(n) UNTIL  n=∅;  ⟹
```

As may be verified from the flow chart, the statements are obeyed at least once. A loop that has to be avoided altogether under certain conditions must be specially protected ≈ say by an IF statement. In such circumstances it may be better to use a WHILE loop.

WHILE LOOP

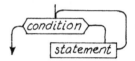

The syntax of the WHILE statement is:

```
WHILE  condition  DO  statement

▶ n := 3;  WHILE  n>∅ DO BEGIN  n:= PRED(n);  WRITELN(n) END;
```

As may be verified from the flow chart, the test for continuance is made before *statement* is obeyed, permitting the loop to be avoided altogether when conditions are not right ((not so with the REPEAT loop)).

A typical use of the WHILE loop is for copying text files. A text file is a file of items separated by spaces and organized into lines   as explained on page 115.

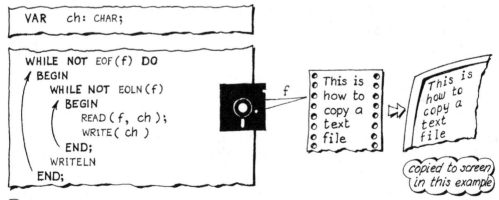

Don't use EOF with keyboard input. Implications of this are explained in chapters 10 and 11.

 **FILTER** — *A PROGRAM TO READ SMALL NUMBERS EMBEDDED IN TEXT ➾ AND ILLUSTRATE REPEAT & WHILE LOOPS*

The READ statement alone cannot be used to read the numbers from the following file because the words and punctuation marks would get in the way. Program *filter* is designed to filter out the extraneous data and abstract just the numbers.

Here is a file to serve as data. It should be typed without pressing RETURN until the final full stop has been typed. ➾

> In 6 months, with luck, I shall have £350, +46.47 in interest but -8.12 in bank charges. That should be enough for a 32k home computer Mk2.

```
  6.00
350.00
 46.47
 -8.12
 32.00
  2.00
```

⇠ Here is the OUTPUT file that the program should create from the INPUT file above.

And here is a program to do the work:

```pascal
PROGRAM  filter ( INPUT, OUTPUT );
   VAR
      ch, sgn: CHAR;  fraction: INTEGER;  number: REAL;
BEGIN
   ch := ' ';        {space}
   WHILE NOT EOLN DO
      BEGIN
         number := 0.0;   fraction := 0;
         sgn := ch;  READ( ch );
         IF ( ch >= '0' ) AND ( ch <= '9' )
            THEN
               BEGIN        { if a digit }
                  REPEAT
                     REPEAT
                        number := 10 * number + ORD( ch ) - ORD( '0' );
                        fraction := fraction * 10;
                        IF NOT EOLN THEN READ( ch );
                     UNTIL ( ( ch < '0' ) OR ( ch > '9' ) ) OR EOLN;
                     IF ( ch = '.' ) AND NOT EOLN
                        THEN
                           BEGIN
                              READ( ch ); fraction := 1
                           END
                  UNTIL ( ( ch < '0' ) OR ( ch > '9' ) ) OR EOLN;
                  IF fraction > 0 THEN number := number / fraction;
                  IF sgn = '-' THEN number := -number;
                  WRITELN ( number : 8 : 2 )
               END    { if a digit }
      END   { while not eoln }
END.
```

a crudity: 🐛 *if you include more than one decimal point, only the last is acted upon; for example 12.3.4 would produce 123.40 without an error report*

The part of any program concerned with input is difficult to keep tidy because of all the checks that have to be made. The program above is particularly untidy but there is a clearer version on page 76 which exploits features of Pascal not yet introduced.

CASE STATEMENT

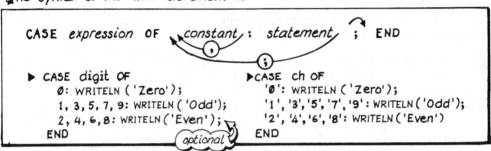

match 1 ⊢ statement1
match 2 ⊢ statement2

The syntax of the CASE statement is:

```
CASE expression OF  constant : statement ; END
                         ,          ;

▶ CASE digit OF              ▶CASE ch OF
    0: WRITELN ('Zero');        '0': WRITELN ('Zero');
    1, 3, 5, 7, 9: WRITELN ('Odd');   '1','3','5','7','9': WRITELN ('Odd');
    2, 4, 6, 8: WRITELN ('Even');     '2','4','6','8': WRITELN ('Even')
  END                           END
```

optional

The *expression* may reduce to a value of any ordered type, typically type INTEGER or CHAR but never REAL. The *expression* and *constants* must be of the same type as one another.

The behaviour of the CASE statement is defined by the flow chart on page 45. When the first precise match is found the corresponding statement is obeyed, none of the others being obeyed. If there is no match at all the behaviour is undefined, so be careful to allow for every possible value that *expression* could reduce to (not always easy to achieve).

Nested CASE statements may be used to represent a *symbol-state table* which is a tidy device for resolving input data. The following table is for decoding Roman numerals with digits X, V and I.

state \ symbol	'X'	'V'	'I'
1	n := 10; state := 2	n := 5; state := 3	n := 1; state := 6
2	n := n+10; state := 2	n := n+5; state := 3	n := n+1; state := 6
3	ok := FALSE	ok := FALSE	n := n+1; state := 4
4	ok := FALSE	ok := FALSE	n := n+1; state := 5
5	ok := FALSE	ok := FALSE	n := n+1; state := 7
6	n := n+8; state := 7	n := n+3; state := 7	n := n+1; state := 5
7	ok := FALSE	ok := FALSE	ok := FALSE

To decode XIV start in state 1 where the arrow is. The first symbol is 'X' so look down from 'X' and find n:=10; state:=2. So set n to 10 and move the arrow to row 2. Now look down from the second symbol, 'I', and find n:=n+1; state:=6. The value in n thus becomes 10+1=11. Move the arrow to row 6. Now look down from the final symbol, 'V', and find n:=n+3; state:=7. The value in n then becomes 11+3=14. Move the arrow to row 7 and notice that any further 'X' or 'V' or 'I' would cause an error (e.g. XIVX).

This table decodes Roman numerals starting with any number of X's and the conventional arrangements of V's and I's:

   I, II, III, IV, V, VI, VII, VIII, IX, X, XI *etc.*

but would treat IIII, for example, as an error by setting ok to FALSE. The table may be extended to cope with M, D, C and L.

SYMBOL~STATE TABLE

```
PROGRAM  roman ( INPUT, OUTPUT );

   VAR  n, state: INTEGER;   symbol: CHAR;   ok: BOOLEAN;
BEGIN  { program }

   state := 1;   ok := TRUE;   n:= 0;
   WHILE NOT EOLN DO
    BEGIN
      READ ( symbol );
      IF ( ( symbol = 'X') OR ( symbol = 'V')) OR ( symbol='I')
          THEN
            CASE state OF
              1: CASE symbol OF
                    'X': BEGIN n := 10; state:=2  END;
                    'V': BEGIN n:= 5; state := 3  END;
                    'I': BEGIN n:= 1; state := 6  END
                 END;
              2: CASE  symbol OF
                    'X': BEGIN  n := n+10; state := 2   END;
                    'V': BEGIN  n := n+5; state := 3   END;
                    'I': BEGIN  n := n+1: state := 6   END
                 END;
              3: CASE symbol OF
                    'X','V': ok := FALSE ;
                    'I': BEGIN n := n+1; state :=4   END
                 END;
              4: CASE  symbol OF
                    'X','V' : ok := FALSE ;
                    'I': BEGIN n := n+ 1; state:=5   END
                 END;
              5: CASE symbol OF
                    'X','V': ok := FALSE ;
                    'I' : BEGIN n:= n+1;  state:=7   END
                 END;
              6: CASE symbol OF
                    'X' BEGIN  n := n+8; state := 7   END;
                    'V' BEGIN  n := n+3; state:= 7   END;
                    'I' BEGIN  n := n+1; state:=5   END
                 END;
              7: ok := FALSE
            END { CASE state}
          ELSE
            BEGIN
              IF ok
                 THEN  WRITELN ( n: 2)
                 ELSE  WRITELN ( ' PECCAVISTI');
              state := 1;   ok := TRUE
            END  { ELSE }
     END { WHILE NOT }

END.  {program}
```

it is nicer to write:
IF symbol IN ['x', 'v', 'I']
as explained in chapter 7

decoded number in n

Note:
terminate final item
with full stop or space
before pressing RETURN

XIV XIVX XX.
14
PECCAVISTI
20

space

EXERCISES

1. Implement the **roman** program. Extend it to cope with:

$$M = 1000, \quad D = 500, \quad C = 100, \quad L = 50.$$

If your Pascal permits interactive working, include prompts for the benefit of the user of the program.

FUNCTIONS AND PROCEDURES

FUNCTION DEFINITION

Pascal does not *provide* a function for returning the area of a circle given the diameter as its actual parameter:

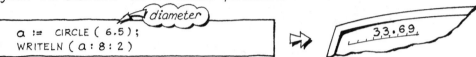

```
a := CIRCLE ( 6.5 );
WRITELN ( a : 8 : 2 )
```
diameter

33.69

But it is easy to *define* such a function:

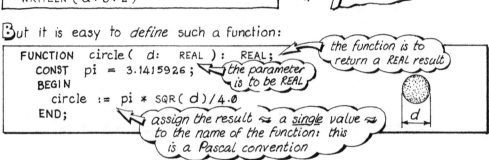

```
FUNCTION  circle( d:   REAL ):   REAL;
   CONST  pi = 3.1415926;
   BEGIN
     circle := pi * SQR( d )/4.0
   END;
```
the function is to return a REAL result

the parameter is to be REAL

assign the result ≈ a single value ≈ to the name of the function: this is a Pascal convention

Thereafter, circle( ) (or CIRCLE( )) may be used in the program just as SQR( ) and TRUNC( ) have been used in earlier examples.

In the top line of the definition, the d says "Do what gets done to me, but use whatever value is put in my place." In the example at the top of this page 6.5 is put in place of d, and so is duly squared, multiplied by 3.1415926, divided by 4.0. The d is a *formal parameter* whereas 6.5 is an *actual parameter*. You could use the name d for a variable (or any other named entity) in the program which invokes area( ) without interference from that function:

```
d := -99;
a := circle( 6.5 );
WRITELN( a, d : 8 : 2 )
```

33.69, -99.00

a
content of d undisturbed

The syntax of a function definition (ignoring, for now, parameters which are themselves functions or procedures) is:

FUNCTION *name* (VAR *name* : *name*$_{type}$): *name*$_{type}$; *block* ;

VAR explained later

type of parameter

type of value to be returned

The item *block* has the structure of a program within a program. The syntax of *block* is properly defined on page 28; this sketch simply illustrates the location of function and procedure definitions in a program.

Function and procedure definitions may have further function and procedure definitions nested within them.

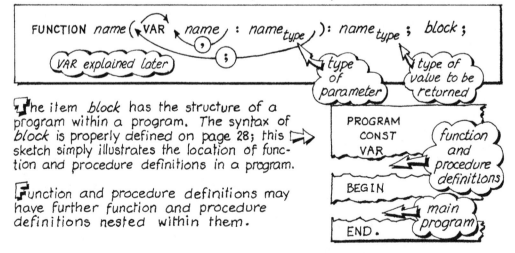

```
PROGRAM
CONST
VAR


BEGIN


END.
```
function and procedure definitions

main program

54

Here is a function for returning the area of a rectangle, given lengths of sides as parameters:

```
FUNCTION  rectangle ( b, d: REAL ): REAL;
   BEGIN  rectangle := b * d   END;
```

And a similar one for the area of a triangle:

```
FUNCTION  triangle (a, b, c: REAL ): REAL;
   VAR    x: REAL;
     BEGIN
        x := ( a + b + c )/2;
        triangle := SQRT ( x * (x-a)*(x-b)*(x-c) )
     END;
```

These three functions (| circle( ), rectangle( ), triangle( ) |) may be invoked from the following program which is a re-designed version of the program on page 17.

```
PROGRAM   shapes2 ( INPUT,  OUTPUT );
   VAR  letter: CHAR;    a, x, y, z: REAL;

   put the three functions here in any order

   BEGIN
      REPEAT
         READ ( letter );
            CASE  letter  OF
               'q', 'Q' :  a := Ø ;
               'r', 'R' :  BEGIN
                             READLN ( x,y );   a := rectangle ( x,y )
                           END;

               't', 'T' :  BEGIN
                             READLN ( x, y, z );  a := triangle ( x,y,z )
                           END;

               'c', 'C' :  BEGIN
                             READLN( x );   a := circle ( x )
                           END
            END;  {CASE letter }
            WRITELN ( 'Area is ',  a: 8:2 )
      UNTIL ( letter = 'Q' ) OR ( letter = 'q' )
   END.
```

```
R  3.5  2
Area is 7.00
C  6.5
Area is 33.69
r  4  6
Area is 24.00
t  3  4  5
Area is 6.00
Quit
Area is 0.00
```

Notice that the functions are invoked with *actual* parameters *x, y, z* whereas *formal* parameters *a, b, c, d* were used in the definitions. Variable *a* in the main program has no connection with formal parameter *a* in function triangle(, ,). Likewise, variable *x* in the main program has no connection with *local* variable *x* in function triangle(, ,). More about this later.

Each function defined here has a different number of parameters. Any fixed number is permissible, but never a variable number as with READ(a), READ(a,b), READ(a, b, c) *etc*. This facility is enjoyed by Pascal alone.

In the above examples all types are REAL, but in general any mixture of types is allowed: *eg.* mixfun (a: REAL; b: INTEGER; c: CHAR): BOOLEAN;

There is no Pascal function for returning a cube root. Here is one defined:

```
FUNCTION cubrt( x: REAL): REAL;
   VAR old, noo: REAL;
      BEGIN
         IF x = Ø THEN cubrt := Ø ELSE
            BEGIN old := 1;
               REPEAT
                  noo := x/SQR(old);
                  old := (noo+old)/2
               UNTIL ABS( x/(noo*noo*noo)-1) < 1E-6 ;
               cubrt := noo
            END
      END;  { of function }
```

exit when $\frac{x}{(guess)^3} \approx 1$

cubrt (-27) returns -3
cubrt (Ø) returns Ø
cubrt (27) returns 3

Basic programmers regretting the absence of SGN( ) may define it; either directly:

```
FUNCTION sgn(x: REAL): INTEGER;
   BEGIN
      IF x > Ø THEN sgn := 1 ELSE
      IF x < Ø THEN sgn := -1 ELSE sgn := Ø
   END;
```

returns 1 if $x > 0$
returns -1 if $x < 0$
returns 0 if $x = 0$

or with cunning:

```
FUNCTION sgn(x: REAL): INTEGER;
   BEGIN sgn := ORD( x > Ø) - ORD( x < Ø) END;
```

works because:
ORD(TRUE)=1, ORD(FALSE)=0

There is no TAN( ) function in Pascal (tangent of an angle measured in radians) but here is one defined:

```
FUNCTION tan( x: REAL): REAL;
   BEGIN
      tan := SIN(x) / COS(x)
   END;
```

$\sin x = p/h$
$\cos x = a/h$
$\tan x = \frac{p}{a} = \frac{p/h}{a/h} = \frac{\sin x}{\cos x}$

Here are functions for the arcsine (the angle, in radians, whose sine is...) and arccosine :

```
FUNCTION arcsin( x: REAL): REAL;
   BEGIN
      IF ABS (x) = 1
         THEN arcsin := x * 1.5707963
         ELSE arcsin := ARCTAN ( x/SQRT(1-SQR(x)))
   END;

FUNCTION arccos(x: REAL): REAL;
   BEGIN
      IF x = Ø
         THEN arccos := 1.5707963
         ELSE arccos := ARCTAN(SQRT(1-SQR(x))/x ) +3.1415926*ORD(x<Ø)
   END;
```

$\pm \pi/2$

$\sin \alpha = x/1$
$\tan \alpha = \frac{x}{\sqrt{1-x^2}}$
$\therefore \alpha = \arctan(x/\sqrt{1-x^2})$

$\cos \alpha = x/1$
$\tan \alpha = \sqrt{1-x^2}/x$
$\therefore \alpha = \arctan(\sqrt{1-x^2}/x)$

$+\pi/2$

$+\pi$ when $x \geqslant 0$

There is more about the arcsin( ) and arccos( ) functions on page 68 .

RECURSION

The highest common factor 《 hcf 》 of 1470 and 693 is 21. In other words 21 is the biggest number that will divide into 1470 and 693 without leaving a remainder in either case. To verify this, factorize both numbers to prime factors:

$$1470 = 2 \times 3 \times 5 \times 7 \times 7$$
$$693 = 3 \times 3 \times 7 \times 11$$

and pair off any common factors ⇆ in this case 3 and 7. The highest common factor 《 also called *gcd*, or greatest common divisor 》 is the product of these; in this case 3 × 7 = 21.

Euclid's method of finding the hcf is more elegant. Find the remainder when 1470 is divided by 693:

$$1470 \quad MOD \quad 693 \quad = \quad 84$$

Because this remainder is not zero, repeat the process substituting the second number for the first and the remainder for the second:

$$693 \quad MOD \quad 84 \quad = \quad 21$$

This remainder is still not zero, so repeat the process:

$$84 \quad MOD \quad 21 \quad = \quad 0$$

This remainder is zero, so the hcf is 21. Nice.

Here is a Pascal function based on Euclid's method:

```
FUNCTION  hcf ( n, m : INTEGER ) : INTEGER ;
   VAR    rem : INTEGER ;                    recursive
   BEGIN                                     invocation
     rem := n MOD m ;
     IF rem = 0 THEN hcf := m ELSE hcf := hcf( m, rem )
   END ;
```

this works both for n ≥ m and m < n

It is easy to see what would happen with hcf(84,21) because rem would become zero making the function return 21. But with hcf(1470,693) rem becomes 84 so the function invokes itself as hcf(693,84). In so doing *rem* becomes 21, therefore the function invokes itself as hcf(84,21). It is as though Pascal provided a fresh copy of the code of the function hcf(,) on each invocation:

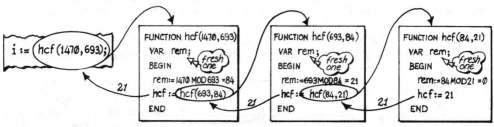

The ability of a function to invoke itself is called *recursion*. There is more about recursion in this and subsequent chapters.

PROCEDURES

When a piece of program is to be used more than once in the same program there is no need for its text to be duplicated; its text may be parcelled as a procedure, given a name, and invoked by that name whenever its text is to be obeyed. Here is a trivial example; a procedure for writing two integers in reverse order of the two parameters:

```
PROCEDURE  reverse( a, b: INTEGER );
  BEGIN
     WRITELN ( b:3 , a:3 )
  END;
```

From the main program this procedure could be invoked thus:

```
x := 1;    y := 100;
reverse ( x, y);
reverse ( 4, 5);
reverse ( 4 * x,  5 * y)
```

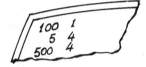

```
100  1
  5  4
500  4
```

The above is silly, but serves to show that the actual parameters may be constants (4 , 5) or expressions (4*x, 5*y) or names of variables (x,y). Every time reverse( ) is invoked its actual parameters are evaluated and these *values* are substituted for the formal parameters *a* and *b*. For this reason *a* and *b* are called "value" parameters.

Instead of writing values in reverse order suppose it were required to exchange the values stored in a pair of integer variables. The following would be no good at all:

```
PROCEDURE  swop( a, b : INTEGER );
  VAR
     tempry : INTEGER ;
  BEGIN
     tempry := a;   a := b;  b := tempry
  END;
```

Suppose it were to be invoked as follows with x containing 1, y containing 100:

```
swop ( x, y )
```

The effect would be to store the values 1 in *a*, 100 in *b*; then to make the swop in *a* and *b*; then to return to the program with x and y unaffected. The procedure is interested only in the *values* of its parameters; swop(4,5) or swop(4*x, 5*y) would have the same non-result.

The solution is to make the parameters into VAR parameters. Writing VAR in front of a parameter gives access to a variable in the invoking program:

```
PROCEDURE  swop( VAR a, b : INTEGER );
  VAR
     tempry : INTEGER;
  BEGIN
     tempry := a;   a := b;  b := tempry
  END;
```

you can now change the contents of variables belonging to the invoking program

Now suppose the procedure were invoked as follows:

```
x:= 1;    y := 100;
swop ( x, y )
WRITELN ( x, y )
```

In simple terms: *put* VAR *in front of those parameters whose values are to be changed by the procedure.*

A more sophisticated concept is that VAR in the procedure heading signifies direct access to the invoking program. The statement a:=b in the procedure signifies x:=y in the invoking program (when invoked as shown above). In the jargon: VAR parameters are *passed by address* or *passed by reference* whereas value parameters are *passed by value* ⇌ the procedure having to set up a local variable to store each value passed.

The following invocations are meaningless with VAR parameters; invocations

```
swop ( 4, 5 );
swop ( 4*x, 5*y )
```
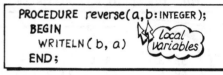

are meaningful if both parameters are names of variables which contain values to be swopped.

A point of possible confusion: the VAR section of a procedure is for declaring variables *local* to that procedure, whereas VAR in the procedure heading signifies reference to *non-local* variables:

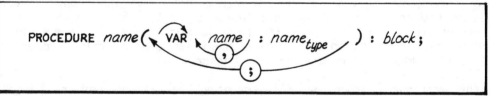

```
PROCEDURE swop(VAR a,b:INTEGER);
  VAR tempry:INTEGER;          non-local
  BEGIN                   local
   tempry:=a; a:=b; b:=tempry
  END;
```

```
PROCEDURE reverse(a,b:INTEGER);
  BEGIN                    local
    WRITELN( b, a )       variables
  END;
```

Here is the syntax of procedure definition (ignoring, for now, parameters which are themselves names of functions).

$$PROCEDURE \; name(\; VAR \; name_{,} : name_{type} \;) : block;$$

The item *block* has the structure of a program within a program. The syntax of *block* is properly defined on page 28.

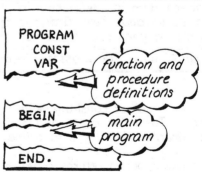

```
PROGRAM
CONST
VAR           function and
              procedure
              definitions
BEGIN         main
              program
END.
```

This diagram shows the location of function and procedure definitions within a program. Each function and procedure definition may have further function and procedure definitions *nested* within it.

RANDOM NUMBERS

Consider the following function:

```
FUNCTION   next ( VAR seed : INTEGER ): INTEGER ;
   CONST    multiplier = 37 ;  increment = 3 ;  cycle = 64 ;
   BEGIN
      next := seed ;
      seed := ( multiplier * seed + increment ) MOD cycle
   END;
```

notice VAR in the heading; an unusual tactic in a function

Invoked with s containing 16 as follows:

```
   s := 16 ;  WRITE ( next ( s ))
```

16

this function must obviously return 16. Furthermore, whenever the function returns 16 it must always change the value stored in *seed* to 19. If the function were again invoked, but with the new setting of s, it would return 19 and change the value in s to 2. Continually invoking next( ) in this way would produce a predetermined sequence of integers running from the initial value given to s :

```
   s := 16;
   FOR i := 1 TO 64 DO  WRITE ( next ( s ): 3)
```

16	19	2	13	36	55	54	17	56	27	42	21	12	63	30	25
32	35	18	29	52	7	6	33	8	43	58	37	28	15	46	41
48	51	34	45	4	23	22	49	24	59	10	53	44	31	62	57
0	3	50	61	20	39	38	1	40	11	26	5	60	47	14	9

A remarkable thing about this sequence is that every value from 0 to 63 occurs precisely once. Furthermore, invoking next( ) for the sixty-fifth time would produce 16, re-starting the identical cycle of integers. In other words the function generates a fixed permutation of the integers 0 to 63, starting from any desired integer.

This technique is much used for generating "random" numbers (strictly *pseudo*-random in deference to their predictability). A cycle of 64 would be inadequate; Grogono (see Bibliography) gives a set of constants to generate a permutation of integers 0 to 65535 :

```
   CONST  multiplier = 25173;  increment = 13849;  cycle = 65536;
```

Choosing a set of constants with the necessary properties is not a trivial exercise. To arrive at 37 and 3 for the cycle of 64 numbers shown above I experimented blindly with prime numbers.

The above function returns a value *and alters the value of the parameter*. The tactic is unusual. Most functions have no need to disturb their parameters, and accordingly make no use of VAR in the headings of their definitions.

In computer simulations and games it is usual to employ random *fractions* in the range 0 ≤ fraction ≤ 1 rather than random integers. This requires a few changes to the function defined opposite:

```
FUNCTION  rnd ( VAR seed : INTEGER ): REAL;          ← formerly INTEGER
   CONST multiplier=25173; increment=13849; cycle=65536;   ← Grogono's constants
   BEGIN
   rnd := seed / cycle;          name changed to rnd()
   seed := (multiplier * seed + increment) MOD cycle      and divisor added
   END;                                                    0.0 ≤ rnd < 1.0
```

This function will not work if MAXINT has a value of less than $2^{31}-1$. But here is an ingeniously modified version which generates a cycle of 32768 fractions even if MAXINT has a value as low as $2^{16}-1$ (32767):

```
FUNCTION  rnd ( VAR seed : INTEGER ): REAL;
   VAR  a, b, c, d : INTEGER;                    0.0 ≤ rnd ≤ 1.0
   BEGIN                                                N.B.
   rnd := seed / 32767;
   a := seed DIV 256;
   b := seed MOD 256;
   c := (( b*93) MOD 256 ) + 13;
   d := ( b*26)+((b*93) DIV 256)+(a*93)+(c DIV 256)+27;
   seed := (( d MOD 128) *256) + (c MOD 256)
   END;
```

Here is a simulation to show how much wiser it is to bet on 7 than any other score if throwing a pair of dice for even money. (An array ≈ see chapter 8 ≈ would make the program simpler.)

```
PROGRAM  bones ( OUTPUT );
   VAR  score, throws, seed, a,b,c,d,e,f,g,h,i,j,k : INTEGER;
              insert first version of rnd( ) here

BEGIN
   seed := 0;  a:=0; b:=0; c:=0; d:=0; e:=0; f:=0;
   g:=0; h:=0; i:=0; j:=0; k:=0;           6*rnd(seed) has
   FOR throws := 1 TO 3600 DO              range 0.0 to under 6.0
      BEGIN  {throws}
      score:= ROUND (1+5*rnd(seed))+ ROUND(1+5* rnd (seed)) ;
      CASE  score OF
      2:  a:= a+1;    12:  k:= k +1;
      3:  b:= b+1;    11:  j:= j +1;
      4:  c:= c+1;    10:  i:= i +1;
      5:  d:= d+1;     9:  h:= h +1;
      6:  e:= e+1;     8:  g:= g +1;
      7:  f:= f+1
      END  {CASE}
   END;  { FOR throws }
   WRITELN ( 2, 3, 4, 5, 6, 7, 8, 9, 10, 11, 12);
   WRITELN (a, b, c, d, e, f, g, h, i, j, k)
END.
```

2	3	4	5	6	7	8	9	10	11	12
89	194	298	396	523	558	532	418	298	202	92
100	200	300	400	500	600	500	400	300	200	100

compare the "ideal" scores

choose suitable format for output device; e.g. a:4, b:4, c:4 etc.

The result is roughly symmetrical about 7. Comparison of results with "ideal" scores is encouraging; see page 68 about a much bigger sample.

LOANS AGAIN

The program on page 15 computes the monthly repayment, m, on a mortgage loan of s at p% compound interest over n years. But here is a more difficult problem; a loan of s is to be repaid at m per month over n years; what rate of interest is being charged?

$$m = \frac{sr(1 + r)^n}{12\left[(1 + r)^n - 1\right]}$$

$$\text{where} \quad r = p \div 100$$

The equation may be solved by trial and error. Guess r; substitute in the formula and compute $m1$. If $m1$ is the same as m the guess was correct. If $m1$ was too small it means r was guessed too low, so multiply r by $m/m1$ to make it bigger and try again. If $m1$ is too big it means r was guessed too high, so multiply r by $m/m1$ to make it smaller and try again. In short; if $m1$ is not close enough to m multiply r by $m/m1$ and try again. Sooner or later r will get close enough to be acceptable as a solution to the equation.

This method works well as long as an increase in one thing implies a corresponding increase (or decrease) in another. It fails if the other fluctuates or there is a discontinuity such as a bankrupt mortgagee.

Here is the program:

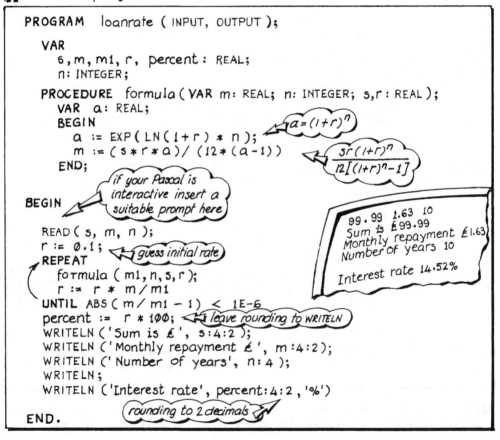

```
PROGRAM   loanrate ( INPUT, OUTPUT );

  VAR
     s, m, m1, r, percent : REAL;
     n: INTEGER;

  PROCEDURE formula ( VAR m: REAL; n: INTEGER; s,r: REAL );
     VAR  a: REAL;
     BEGIN
        a := EXP ( LN ( 1+r ) * n );          ← a = (1+r)ⁿ
        m := ( s*r*a ) / ( 12 * ( a-1 ) )     ← sr(1+r)ⁿ / 12[(1+r)ⁿ-1]
     END;
                    if your Pascal is
                    interactive insert a
  BEGIN             suitable prompt here

     READ ( s, m, n );
     r := 0.1;   ← guess initial rate
     REPEAT
        formula ( m1, n, s, r );
        r := r * m / m1
     UNTIL ABS ( m / m1 - 1 ) < 1E-6
     percent := r * 100;   ← leave rounding to WRITELN
     WRITELN ('Sum is £ ', s:4:2 );
     WRITELN ('Monthly repayment £ ', m:4:2 );
     WRITELN (' Number of years', n:4 );
     WRITELN;
     WRITELN ('Interest rate', percent:4:2 , '%')
                    rounding to 2 decimals
  END.
```

```
99.99  1.63  10
Sum is £99.99
Monthly repayment £1.63
Number of years 10

Interest rate 14.52%
```

FUNCTION NAMES AS PARAMETERS

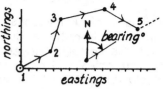

Here are the statements of a program to compute northings and eastings of points on the ground, given the compass bearing at each point and the paced distance from the previous point 〔 a traverse 〕 .

```
BEGIN
    northing := 0; easting := 0;    ←origin at point 1
    WHILE NOT EOF(f)        INPUT file        zero at point 1        name of
        BEGIN                                                         a function
            READLN ( f, bearing, distance );
            northing := northing + projection( bearing, distance, cosine);
            easting := easting + projection( bearing, distance, sine);
            WRITELN ( northing:10:2, easting:10:2)                   name of
        END { WHILE }                                                a function
END. { program }
```

Here is the definition of projection(, ,) :

may not be a VAR parameter

```
FUNCTION projection( bng, dist: REAL; FUNCTION ratio(x:REAL):REAL): REAL;
BEGIN
    projection := dist * ratio( bng )      defines the third
END;                                        formal parameter
```

And here are the definitions of the functions whose names are used as *actual* parameters of projection(, ,):

```
FUNCTION sine ( b: REAL): REAL;
    BEGIN sine := SIN( 3.1415926 * b/ 180 ) END;

FUNCTION cosine ( b: REAL): REAL;
    BEGIN cosine := COS (3.1415926 * b/ 180) END;
```

Notice how the third formal parameter of projection(, ,) is defined:

FUNCTION ratio (x : REAL) : REAL

says the actual parameter is to be the name of a user-defined function | *says the user-defined function is to have a REAL parameter* | *says the user-defined function is to return a REAL result*

where x serves only to mark the place of a parameter, keeping the syntax consistent with that of a function definition.

To complete the picture, here is the start of the program:

```
PROGRAM traverse ( f, OUTPUT );
    VAR northing, easting: REAL;
```
put function definitions here, followed by the main program

The problem is to find a compiler on which this works. Many compilers refuse to allow names of functions to be used as parameters, and I can't say I blame them. The only sensible applications of this facility I have so far seen concern mathematical integration.

...BREATHE OUT!

FORWARD REFERENCES

In any *block* the CONST and VAR declarations precede the BEGIN and END which enclose the statements themselves. This enforced order implies that the compiler never has to handle a statement containing *constants* or variables it does not know about. The appearance of an un-declared constant or variable would evoke an error message during compilation.

The same logic applies to *subprograms* (*i.e.* functions and procedures). An error message is evoked if the compiler meets an invocation of a subprogram it does not know about. It is the programmer's responsibility to see that definitions are properly ordered.

```
PROGRAM   demo( INPUT, OUTPUT );
  VAR a, b, c : REAL;
  PROCEDURE   ring( VAR area, circumf: REAL; diam:REAL );
    BEGIN
      circumf := 3.14 * diam ;               the compiler does not know
      area := circle( diam )                 about function circle( )
    END                                      on reaching here

  FUNCTION   circle( d: REAL): REAL;
    BEGIN  circle := 3.14 * SQR(d) / 4  END;
```

An obvious solution to this problem is to re-order the input so that the function circle( ) is defined before the procedure ring(,,). But there is a less drastic solution (*drastic* remembering that real-life programs are longer than the trivial example programs shown here) :

- leave the offending subprogram where it is, but simplify its heading by removing all parameters

- insert the full heading where it ought to be ≈ *i.e. before* the subprogram that invokes it

- add the predefined word FORWARD after the full heading:

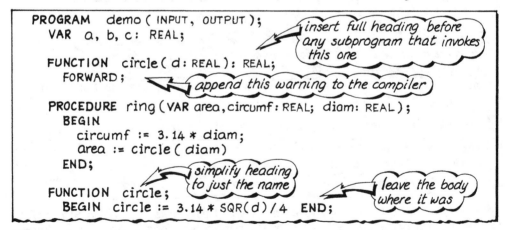

```
PROGRAM   demo ( INPUT, OUTPUT );           insert full heading before
  VAR a, b, c: REAL;                        any subprogram that invokes
                                            this one
  FUNCTION   circle( d: REAL ): REAL;
    FORWARD ;              append this warning to the compiler

  PROCEDURE   ring (VAR area, circumf: REAL; diam: REAL );
    BEGIN
      circumf := 3.14 * diam;
      area := circle( diam)
    END;                  simplify heading
                          to just the name           leave the body
  FUNCTION   circle;                                 where it was
    BEGIN  circle := 3.14 * SQR(d) / 4   END;
```

The only other forward reference allowed in Pascal is to do with pointers in linked lists as described in chapter 12.

LOCAL VARIABLES
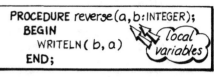
FRESH ON EACH INVOCATION, EVAPORATING ON RETURN

The following sketches were used on page 59 to distinguish those variables that are *local* to a procedure from those that are not:

```
PROCEDURE swop(VAR a,b:INTEGER);
   VAR tempry
   BEGIN
      tempry:=a; a:=b; b:=tempry
   END;
```
local   non-local variables

```
PROCEDURE reverse(a,b:INTEGER);
   BEGIN
      WRITELN(b,a)
   END;
```
local variables

Local variables are created as a procedure is invoked. Then current values of any *value* parameters are copied into the local variables created for them. For example the invocation:

```
      reverse( 4 , 5 );
```

would cause 4 to be copied into local variable *a* and 5 into local variable *b*.

The procedure is then put to work. On completion, when control returns to the invoking program, all local variables are forgotten, their contents being lost forever. *But the local variables do not evaporate until control returns to the invoking program.* This behaviour is essential to re- cursion as illustrated by this hackneyed example of "factorial":

```
FUNCTION  factorial ( number: INTEGER): INTEGER;
   VAR   n: INTEGER;
   BEGIN                          local variable n  □
      n := number;
      IF n = 1 THEN  factorial := 1
               ELSE  factorial := n * factorial (n-1)
   END;
```

Trace the behaviour of the function for the invocation m := factorial(4):

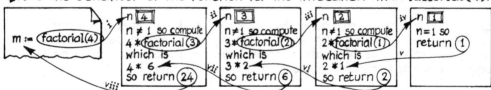

```
        i   n 4              ii  n 3              iii n 2              iv  n 1
m := factorial(4)  n ≠ 1 so compute  n ≠ 1 so compute  n ≠ 1 so compute  n=1 so
                   4 * factorial(3)  3 * factorial(2)  2 * factorial(1)  return 1
                   which is         which is         which is                v
                   4 * 6            3 * 2            2 * 1
              viii so return 24  vii so return 6  vi so return 2
```

Notice that the first copy of *factorial* remembers the value 4 in local variable *n* until the 24 is returned to *m*. Similarly the second copy remembers the 3 until the 6 is returned to the first copy, and so on. A local variable is local to the current copy; at one instant during the execution depicted above there would be *four* distinct copies of local variable *n*.

It was *not* necessary to declare VAR n as above; value parameters are auto- matically declared as local variables:

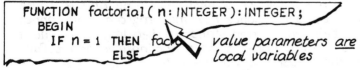

```
FUNCTION  factorial ( n: INTEGER): INTEGER;
   BEGIN
      IF n = 1 THEN  fac      value parameters are
               ELSE           local variables
```

65

SIDE EFFECTS

Here is an alternative to the random number generator on page 61 :

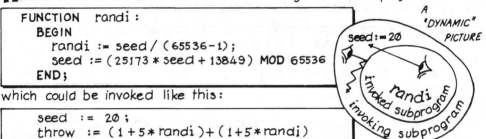

```
FUNCTION  randi :
  BEGIN
    randi := seed / (65536-1);
    seed := (25173 * seed + 13849) MOD 65536
  END;
```

A "DYNAMIC" PICTURE

which could be invoked like this :

```
    seed  := 20 ;
    throw := (1 + 5 * randi) + (1 + 5 * randi)
```

The example works because the computer can "see" the variable named *seed* whilst working inside function randi. Furthermore randi can cause a change in the value stored in the variable named *seed*. An invoked subprogram can see outwards to its invoking program but cannot be seen *by* it.

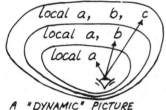

A "DYNAMIC" PICTURE

When a subprogram refers to variable *a* it means the *local* variable *a*. If there is no local variable *a* the eye looks outwards to the invoking subprogram ((possibly a recursive copy of itself)) and refers to the *local* variable *a* in that subprogram. If there is no local variable *a* the eye looks outwards...

The same principle applies to all named entities : variables, constants, functions, procedures, files and types.

When a subprogram *changes* the value stored in a variable declared outside itself the subprogram is said to have a *side effect*. Function randi has a side effect; it changes the value stored in *seed* which is a variable declared outside randi.

Side effects are often caused by accident. Making repeated use of variables with names like *a, b, c* whilst forgetting to declare them locally is a potential source of trouble; some books on Pascal advocate the use of long names for variables so as to avoid this danger.

When programs are small it may be clearest to make all variables global. When *sets* are used ((sets are described in the next chapter)) it may be the only sane approach to make all set variables global. And in long programs it may make sense to define a few global variables to be referred to from inside procedures. But it is bad practice to employ side effects sporadically or carelessly.

Opposite is the skeleton of a typical program. Borders are drawn around subprograms to emphasize the nested structure. The notes explain what variables are available in each layer of nesting, those able to cause side effects being pointed out. Notice how the program itself appears as a subprogram ((albeit with a non-standard heading to define the input and output files and a non-standard ending involving a full stop)) nested within the "Pascal environment".

PASCAL ENVIRONMENT : standard files (INPUT, OUTPUT), types (REAL etc.)
functions (SQR( ) etc.), procedures (WRITE( ) etc.), constants (TRUE, FALSE)

PROGRAM twigs (INPUT, OUTPUT);
  VAR a, b, c: REAL;

  PROCEDURE lining (p, q: REAL; VAR x, y : REAL);
    VAR a, b : REAL;

    PROCEDURE chick(p: REAL; VAR x: REAL);
      VAR a, d : REAL;
      BEGIN in these statements you may:
      ✻ employ a, d, p belonging to chick
      ✻ employ b belonging to lining, c belonging to twigs ⟸ potential side effects
      ✻ employ x to return result via invocation of chick
      ✻ employ y "   "   "   "   "   " lining
      ✻ invoke chick or lining recursively
      ✻ use all Pascal files, types, functions, procedures, constants
      END;

    PROCEDURE egg (p: REAL; VAR x : REAL);
      VAR a, e :
      BEGIN in these statements you may:
      ✻ employ a, e, p belonging to egg
      ✻ employ b belonging to lining, c belonging to twigs ⟸ potential side effects
      ✻ employ x to return result via invocation of egg
      ✻ employ y "   "   "   "   "   " lining
      ✻ invoke chick (for chick to invoke egg you need FORWARD)
      ✻ invoke egg or lining recursively
      ✻ use all Pascal files, types, functions, procedures, constants
      END;

    BEGIN {lining} in these statements you may:
    ✻ employ a, b, p, q belonging to lining
    ✻ employ c belonging to twigs
    ✻ employ x, y to return results via invocations of lining potential side effects
    ✻ invoke chick, egg
    ✻ invoke lining recursively
    ✻ use all Pascal files, types, functions, procedures, constants
    END;

  BEGIN {twigs} in the main program you may
  ✻ employ a, b, c belonging to twigs
  ✻ invoke lining
  ✻ use all Pascal files, types, functions, procedures, constants
  END.

EXERCISES

1. To appreciate the range of results generated by the arcsin( ) and arccos( ) functions defined on page 56, write a program to tabulate results given parameters from −1 to +1 in increments of 0·1. For example the essence of such a program could be the statement:

```
FOR n := −1Ø TO 1Ø DO
   WRITELN ( n/1Ø:6:2, arcsin(n/1Ø):6:2, arccos(n/1Ø):6:2)
```

2. Implement the program named *bones* on page 61. If you have ample computer time to spare increase the number of dice throws from 3600 to 32768 to see if the scores turn out to be closer to the "ideal" ones.

3. Implement the program named *loanrate* on page 62. As with the previous *loans* program this one fails if the rate is zero. Make good this defect. If your Pascal system permits interactive input make the program prompt its user for each item of data required.

7

TYPES AND SETS

STANDARD TYPES

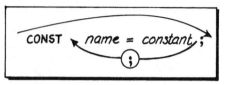

REAL, INTEGER, CHAR, BOOLEAN
~ A SUMMARY ~

Constants of standard types may be defined in the CONST section of any block. The type of each constant does not have to be declared; it is recognizable by its "literal" form:

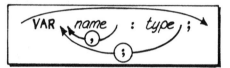

```
CONST pi = 3.14;  increment = 1;  star = '*';
```

decimal point, therefore pi is REAL

no decimal point, therefore INTEGER

apostrophes; therefore * is of type CHAR

or by being set equal to some previously-named constant:

```
p = pi;  stella = star;  verily = TRUE;  decrement = –increment;
```

no expressions; the limit of complexity is x=-y

The type of each *variable* must be declared in the VAR section of the block in which it is to be used:

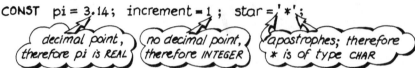

The type of each *parameter* must be declared in a procedure heading or function heading.

```
FUNCTION mix (r: REAL; i: INTEGER; c: CHAR): BOOLEAN;
   VAR s: REAL;  j: INTEGER;  letter: CHAR;  ok: BOOLEAN
```

Arithmetic involving standard types is described in chapter 4; in particular the mixture of REAL and INTEGER types in an *expression* and conversion of a result of one type to the other.

Expressions involving type CHAR or operators NOT, AND, OR reduce to a Boolean result.

The following concerns *ordinal values*:

- An integer has an ordinal value equal to itself (| ORD(6) is 6 |) and therefore has predecessor and successor (| PRED(6) is 5; SUCC (6) is 7 |)

- An item of type REAL has no ordinal value

- An item of type CHAR has an ordinal value such that ORD('A') < ORD('B') *etc.* and ORD('1') – ORD('0') is 1, ORD('2') – ORD('0') is 2 *etc.*

- When writing a *condition* the ORD( ) is implied by omission; thus ORD('I') < ORD('J') may be simplified to 'I' < 'J'. But recall that SUCC ('I') is not necessarily 'J', nor is ORD ('J') – ORD('I') necessarily 1.

70

TYPE DEFINITION *OF ENUMERATIONS, SUBRANGES AND SETS OF THESE*

The programmer may devise and define simple types other than the four standard types. These definitions may be given in the TYPE section of the relevant block. The TYPE section comes between the CONST and VAR sections as illustrated further down this page.

The syntax of the TYPE section (omitting *structured types* which are dealt with from the next chapter onwards) is shown here. ⇨

The three types are called *enumerated types, subrange types* and *set types*.

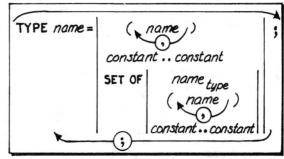

Here is an example of an enumerated type and two subrange types:

```
PROGRAM  dodo( INPUT, OUTPUT );
   CONST  pi = 3.14;                        enumerated type
   TYPE   daytype = ( mon, tue, wed, thu, fri, sat, sun);
          weekdaytype = mon..fri ;          subrange types
          dicetype = 2..12
```

Subsequently the names *daytype, weekdaytype, dicetype* may be used for the definition of variables in the same manner as REAL, INTEGER, CHAR and BOOLEAN. ⇨

```
VAR  x: REAL;
     today: daytype;
     throw, score: dicetype;
PROCEDURE  egg( VAR d: daytype);
```

Alternatively, the definition may be omitted from the TYPE section but included in the VAR section:

```
PROGRAM  dodo( INPUT, OUTPUT );
   CONST  pi = 3.14;
   TYPE   daytype = ( mon, tue, wed, thu, fri, sat, sun) ;
   VAR    x :
          today: mon..fri ;         type definitions moved
          throw, score: 2..12       to the VAR section
```

but such freedom is not permitted in headings of procedures or functions:

```
PROCEDURE  egg ( VAR d: daytype );
```
type of parameter must have been defined in a TYPE section

Enumerations and subranges find application in program control, offering an automatic check on range and scope:

```
WHILE  throw >= score DO  simulate ( throw, score);
CASE today OF
   mon, tue, wed, thu, fri : WRITE ('Work');
   sat, sun : WRITE ('Play')
END {CASE}
```
error message evoked if either variable runs out of range

ENUMERATED TYPES

Here is the definition of two enumerated types and corresponding variables:

```
TYPE   days = ( mon, tue, wed, thu, fri, sat, sun );
       status = ( wedded, unwed );

VAR   today, tomorrow : days
```

> 'wedded' not 'wed' because every name in these enumerations must be unique

You cannot read or write items of enumerated type:

```
READ ( today, tomorrow);
WRITE ( fri, today );
```

You *can* assign values to variables of enumerated type:

```
today := mon;
tomorrow := today;
```

but not if variable and value belong to different enumerations:

```
today := unwed;
```

And you *can't* do arithmetic on them:

```
today := sat + sun
```

Constants of enumerated type have *ordinal values* counting from zero:

```
WRITELN ( ORD (mon), ORD (tue), ORD (sun) );
```

▷ | 0 1 6 |

which implies predecessors and successors:

```
today := PRED ( sun);
tomorrow := SUCC ( today);
WRITELN ( ORD(today), ORD(tomorrow));
```

▷ | 5 6 |

but the first constant has no predecessor and the last has no successor:

```
today := PRED ( mon);
tomorrow := SUCC ( sun );
```

For all items in Pascal which have ordinal values it is allowable to omit the ORD( ) from Boolean expressions:

```
IF ORD (today) > ORD (mon) THEN sayso ;
IF today > mon THEN sayso
```

> the effect of these two statements is identical

Type BOOLEAN is an enumerated type supplied automatically by the Pascal processor:

```
TYPE
    BOOLEAN = ( FALSE, TRUE )
```

so it follows that ORD(FALSE) is zero, ORD(TRUE) is unity, and FALSE < TRUE .

72

SUBRANGES OF ENUMERATIONS, INTEGER & CHAR

Here is the definition of variables of several subranges:

```
TYPE   daytype = ( mon, tue, wed, thu, fri, sat, sun );
VAR    weekday : mon..fri ;        ◄─┤ subrange of daytype
       throw, score: 2..12 ;       ▷─┤ subranges of INTEGER
       musketeer : 1..3;
       grade : 'A' .. 'D'          ◄─┤ subrange of CHAR
```

A subrange may be defined comprising any type which has an *ordinal value*. This precludes subranges of type REAL.

```
VAR    price = 1.99 .. 5.99      ─►✗ of REAL
```

Subranges of enumerations are subject to the restrictions applying to the enumerated type itself. Thus items of type *mon..fri* cannot be read or written, cannot have arithmetic done on them, cannot be assigned to variables except those of type *mon..fri* and *daytype* ⟨ where *daytype* is the *super-range* of which *mon..fri* is the subrange, hence compatible ⟩.

Constants of a subrange of *any* possible type have the same ordinal values as they do in the super-range. Thus in the subrange *sat..sun*, having *daytype* as its super-range, the values ORD(sat) and ORD(sun) would be 5 and 6 respectively; not 0 and 1.

When the super-range of a subrange is of type INTEGER, values of the subrange may be treated as integers. Such treatment may include reading, writing and integer arithmetic:

```
READ ( throw);
score := SQR ( throw);
WRITE ( score);
```

Furthermore, values from different subranges are interchangeable:

```
musketeer := score + 2     ◄─┤ -MAXINT .. MAXINT
            ↙ 1..3    ↙ 2..12
```

Nevertheless a check is made on the bounds of each variable before its value is updated ⟨ by assignment or READ( ) *etc.* ⟩. This automatic restriction to declared bounds is the purpose of subranges. It saves the programmer adding frequent and distracting checks of the form **IF** (score > 12) **OR** (score < 2) **THEN** WRITE ('Bounds exceeded on SCORE'). In a well-written program you would see **VAR** score : 2..12 rather than **VAR** score: INTEGER.

When the super-range of a subrange is of type CHAR, values of the subrange may be treated as characters. This treatment may include reading, writing and employment in Boolean expressions:

```
READ( grade );
IF grade <= 'B'
  THEN   WRITE ('Well done!')
  ELSE   WRITE ( grade, ' will have to do')
```

SET TYPE AND SET VARIABLES

In general terms, a *set* is a collection of items of the same type. In Pascal you may create and name sets for keeping track of the items of any *ordered* type (not REAL or "structured"). "Keeping track" means recording whether each possible item is present or not.

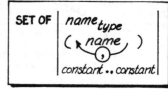

Here is the definition of an enumerated type, followed by a *set type* having *daytype* as its "base type":

```
TYPE
    daytype = (mon, tue, wed, thu, fri, sat, sun );
    dayset = SET OF daytype
```

and here is the definition of two variables for keeping track of sets of days in the manner depicted below:

```
VAR
    washdays, bathdays: dayset;
```

At some time or other during execution of the program the two variables might look like this :

washdays ~mon tue wed thu fri sat sun~   *i.e.* mon wed fri

bathdays ~mon tue wed~ thu fri ~sat sun~   *i.e.* mon thu fri

showing how the information held by a *set* variable comprises one logical value (present or not) for every possible item of the set.

As when defining enumerations and subranges, it is allowable to abbreviate by moving type definitions to the VAR section:

```
TYPE
    daytype = (mon, tue, wed, thu, fri, sat, sun);
VAR
    washdays, bathdays : SET OF daytype
```

or omit the TYPE section altogether:

```
VAR
    washdays, bathdays : SET OF (mon, tue, wed, thu, fri, sat, sun);
```

Here is a VAR section which defines several *set* variables:

```
VAR
    washdays, bathdays : SET OF (mon, tue, wed, thu, fri, sat, sun);
    teaset : SET OF CHAR ;
    letters : SET OF 'A'..'Z' ;
    digits : SET OF '0'..'9' ;
    dice : SET OF 2..12
```

the full SET OF CHAR depends on the installation

SET OF INTEGER is too big for some installations

dice (2 3 4 5 6 7 8 9 10 11 12)   *i.e. depicted full*

digit ( )   *i.e. depicted empty*

74

SET CONSTRUCTORS AND OPERATIONS

A *set constructor* specifies a *set* which may then be assigned to an appropriate variable or manipulated by set operators or both. A *set constructor* may be considered as a *set constant*.

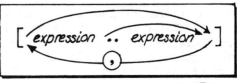

[*expression* .. *expression*]

▶ [2*3..3*3, 5+6, 5] *identical sets*
▶ [5,6,7,8,9, 11]

A set may be emptied thus:

    dice := [ ] ;

∅ [ ] dice

all these terms are valid in subrange 2..12

Or assigned to thus:

    dice := [2*3..3*3, 5+6, 5];

6 7 8 9 11 5 dice

The *union* of two sets is signified by a plus sign:

    dice := [2..5] + [4..6];

dice 2 3 4 5 6   ∪ +

The *intersection* is signified by an asterisk:

    dice := [2..5] * [4..6];

dice 2 3 4 5 6   ∩ *

The *difference* of two sets is signified by a minus sign: −

    dice := [2..5] − [4..6];
    dice := [4..6] − [2..5];

dice 2 3 4 5 6   dice 6 5 2 4 3

Decisions may be based on sets. The comparator IN or >= or <= or = or <> in conjunction with *set* variables or constructors makes a Boolean expression.

Inclusion of a single item in a set may be investigated with IN:

    WRITELN(6 IN [4..6], 6 IN [2..5]);

TRUE FALSE   ∈ IN

One set *contains* another; use >=

    WRITELN ([2..12] >= [3..5]);
    WRITELN ([3..5] >= [2..12]);

TRUE FALSE   ⊇ >=

One set *is contained by* another; use <=

    WRITELN ([3..5] <= [2..12]);
    WRITELN ([2..12] <= [3..5]);

TRUE FALSE   ⊆ <=

One set *is identical to* another; use = or <>

    WRITELN ([3..5] = [5,4,3]);
    WRITELN ([3..5] <> [4,5,3])

TRUE FALSE   ≡

Program *filter* on page 49 reads the INPUT file, abstracting and writing on the OUTPUT file any numbers recognized. The version below has the same specification. It is longer than the earlier version but probably easier to follow because it is less tortuous. Procedures are used in the simplest possible way, working only on global variables.

```
PROGRAM   filter2 ( INPUT, OUTPUT );
   VAR     state : ( ignoring, pending, reading );      ◁ enumerated type
           fraction : 0 .. MAXINT;                      ◁ subrange
           ch: CHAR;   positive: BOOLEAN;   number: REAL;

   PROCEDURE  initialize;
     BEGIN
        state := ignoring;   positive := TRUE;
        number := 0;         fraction := 0
     END;

   PROCEDURE  display;   { then initialize }
     BEGIN
        IF fraction > 0 THEN number := number / fraction;
        IF NOT positive THEN number := -number;
        WRITELN ( number : 10 : 2 );
        initialize
     END;

   PROCEDURE  accumulate;   { & set state to reading }
     BEGIN
        number := 10 * number + ORD(ch) - ORD('0');
        fraction := 10 * fraction;
        state := reading
     END;

   PROCEDURE  negate;   { & set state to pending }
     BEGIN
        positive := FALSE;   state := pending
     END;
```

try this program with the data shown on page 49

state \ symbol	IN ['0'..'9']	'.'	'-'	others
ignoring:	accumulate & set to reading	ignore	negate & set pending	ignore
pending:		initialize		
reading:		fraction:=1	display & initialize	

```
BEGIN  { program }
   initialize;
   WHILE NOT EOLN DO
      BEGIN {WHILE}
         READ( ch );
         CASE state OF

      ignoring: IF ch = '-'
                THEN negate
                ELSE IF ch IN ['0'..'9']
                        THEN accumulate;

      pending:  IF ch IN ['0'..'9']
                THEN accumulate
                ELSE initialize;

      reading:  IF ch = '.'
                THEN fraction := 1
                ELSE IF ch IN ['0'..'9']
                        THEN accumulate
                        ELSE display

      END { CASE }
   END { WHILE };
   IF state = reading THEN display
END.
```

crude logic: any character acts as terminator e.g. $-8-9 would produce: -8.00 9.00*

catch number if at very end of input file

 **A GAME ≈ TO ILLUSTRATE SUBRANGES AND THE MANIPULATION OF SETS**

The computer thinks of a four-digit number having no two digits alike. You type a guess and are told the number of bulls (direct hits) and number of cows (digits in the target but not directly hit). For example with a target of 5734 a guess of 0755 scores 1 bull and 2 cows. Keep guessing until you score four bulls.

```
PROGRAM  mooo ( INPUT, OUTPUT );
  TYPE  playtype = 'Ø'..'9';
        seedtype = Ø.. 65535;
        scoretype = Ø..4;
  VAR   pool, target : SET OF playtype;
        a, b, c, d : playtype;
        seed : seedtype;
        bulls, cows : scoretype;
```

pool

'Ø' '1'
'2' '6'
'8' '9'

e.g.

'5' '7'
'3' '4'

target

```
  FUNCTION  random : REAL;
    BEGIN
      random := seed / 65536;
      seed := ( 25173 * seed + 13849) MOD 65536;
    END; {random}
```

6, not 5, so that result is always less than 1.0

return a random number in range 0.0 ⩽ random < 1.0

```
  FUNCTION  unique : playtype;
    VAR   ch : CHAR;
    BEGIN
      REPEAT
        ch := CHR (TRUNC (1Ø * random) + ORD ('Ø'));
      UNTIL ch IN pool;
      unique := ch;
      pool := pool - [ch];
      target := target + [ ch ]
    END; { unique }
```

set difference

set union

remove a random digit from 'pool' & put it in 'target'

```
  PROCEDURE  try ( thisone : CHAR );
    VAR   ch : CHAR;
    BEGIN
      READ ( ch );
      IF ch IN target
         THEN IF  ch = thisone
                 THEN   bulls := SUCC (bulls)
                 ELSE   cows := SUCC (cows)
    END; { try}
```

read next digit and update count of bulls or cows if appropriate

First enter seed;
35109

1234
Ø Bulls & 1 Cows

5678
1 Bulls & Ø Cows

5990
2 Bulls & Ø Cows

```
BEGIN { PROGRAM }
  WRITELN ('First enter seed; then keep guessing');
  READLN (seed);
  pool := ['Ø'..'9'];  target := [ ];
  a := unique; b := unique; c := unique; d := unique;
  REPEAT
    bulls := Ø;  cows := Ø;
    try(a);  try(b);   try(c);   try(d);
    WRITELN (bulls:1, 'Bulls &':8, cows:2, 'Cows':5);
    READLN
  UNTIL bulls = 4 ;
END. { PROGRAM }
```

full set   *empty set*

create target abcd

4 Bulls & Ø Cows

77

EXERCISES

1. Extend program *filter2* on page 76 to cope with numbers expressed in scientific format:

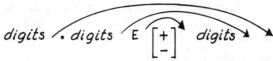

$$digits \; . \; digits \; E \; \begin{bmatrix} + \\ - \end{bmatrix} \; digits$$

This exercise involves extending the symbol-state table.

2. Implement the game of *mooo* on page 77. Improve the game by making the program:

- offer a new game each time a game has been concluded

- stop the game, and count it as a win for the computer, if the target number has not been guessed correctly after ten tries

- keep separate account of the number of wins by the player and number of wins by computer; display these scores on the screen.

8

ARRAYS AND STRINGS

INTRODUCING ARRAYS

Variables of standard type so far encountered have been independent little boxes:

```
VAR   x : REAL;  i, j : INTEGER;  alive : BOOLEAN;  cyfer : CHAR;
```

x ☐   i ☐   j ☐   alive ☐   cyfer ☐   ← *ordinary variables of standard types*

and so have variables of *enumerated* and *subrange* type:

```
TYPE   daytype = (mon, tue, wed, thu, fri, sat, sun);
VAR    today : daytype;  workday : mon..fri;  throw : 2..12;
```

today ☐   workday ☐   throw ☐   ← *ordinary variables of enumerated & subrange types*

But it is also possible to declare variables which are *arrays* of such little boxes:

```
TYPE   daytype = (mon, tue, wed, thu, fri, sat, sun);
       session = (morn, aft, eve);
VAR    vector : ARRAY [1..3] OF REAL;
       roster : ARRAY [mon..fri, session] OF BOOLEAN;
```

← *arrays* →

		morn]	aft]	eve]
vector [1]		roster[mon,			
vector [2] 16·5		roster[tue,		✓	
vector [3] 17·5		roster[wed,			✗
		roster[thu,			
		roster[fri,			

this component is vector [3]

this component is roster[thu, eve]

The little boxes of an array are called *components* : the contents of the square brackets are called *subscripts*. The *base type* of an array is the type of little box of which the array is composed ((only one type of component in any one array)).

Components may be employed in the same way as variables of the base type:

```
vector [2] := 16·5;  READ (vector [3]);
roster [tue, aft] := TRUE;  WRITE (roster[tue, aft]);
roster [wed, eve] := NOT roster [tue, aft];
```

However, there is no merit in using components as though they were ordinary variables; arrays are useful because *subscripts may be variables or expressions which indicate successive components*. Watch this:

```
FOR   day := mon TO fri DO
  FOR   time := morn TO eve DO
    roster [day, time] := FALSE;
FOR i := 1 TO 3 DO vector[i] := 0
```

set all components of roster to FALSE and all components of vector to zero

assuming a preceding VAR section to declare i : 1..3 and day : mon..fri and time : morn..eve

SYNTAX OF ARRAY DECLARATIONS

The arrays depicted opposite could be declared after first naming and defining their types:

```
TYPE   daytype = (mon, tue, wed, thu, fri, sat, sun);
       session = (morn, aft, eve);
       vectortype = ARRAY [1..3] OF REAL;
       rostertype = ARRAY [mon..fri, session] OF BOOLEAN;

VAR    vector : vectortype;
       roster : rostertype;
```

enumerated types

array types

array variables defined in terms of array types

The syntax of *array type* is:

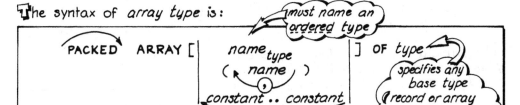

must name an ordered type

PACKED ARRAY [name *type* / (name) / constant .. constant] OF *type*

specifies any base type (record or array types not precluded)

The syntax for referring to a component of an array is:

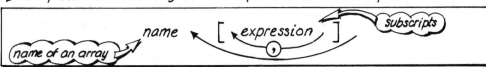

name [expression]

subscripts

name of an array

Arrays are manipulated by altering the subscripts of components as illustrated opposite. But there is an important exception; a copy of the *entire* content of one array may be assigned to another *of the same type* in a single operation:

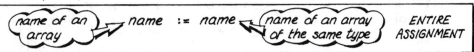

name of an array   name := name   *name of an array of the same type*   ENTIRE ASSIGNMENT

where "same type" means a type with the *same name*. A type which has the same specification but different name is not equivalent:

```
TYPE   atype = ARRAY [1..3] OF REAL;
VAR    a, b : atype;  c: ARRAY [1..3] OF REAL;

       a := b  (same named type)      a := c  (same specification)
```

An exception to the above is `PACKED ARRAY [ ] OF CHAR` for which, in some Pascals, equivalence is not demanded. Change REAL to CHAR above and `a := c` would be permitted.

A two-dimensional array such as *roster* is really an *array of arrays*. The following syntax would be allowable but is unnecessarily clumsy:

```
TYPE   rostertype = ARRAY [mon..fri] OF ARRAY [session] OF BOOLEAN;
       roster [day] [time] := FALSE
```

AREA OF A POLYGON

Consider the diagram on the right : ⟹
The spotted area is given by A_{ij} where

$$A_{ij} = \tfrac{1}{2} (X_i Y_j - X_j Y_i)$$
$$= \tfrac{1}{2} (2 \times 3 - 2.5 \times 1) = 1.75$$

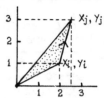

⟸ The same formula may be used for computing the area on the left. But this area turns out to be *negative* :

$$A_{ij} = \tfrac{1}{2} (X_i Y_j - X_j Y_i)$$
$$= \tfrac{1}{2} (3 \times 2.5 - 5 \times 4) = -6.25$$

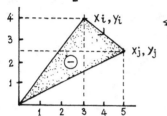

The formula may be applied to sequential sides of a polygon, and the triangular areas summed to give the area shown here ⟹

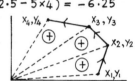

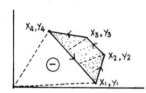

But if the polygon is *closed*, as shown on ⟸ the left, the sum of the areas will be the area enclosed.

The bounded surface must be kept to the *left* of each arrow; the sides of the figure should not cross each other as in a figure of eight.

Here is a program by which to input **coordinates** of boundary points and compute the area enclosed:

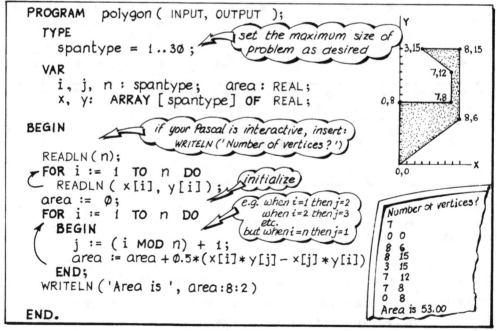

```
PROGRAM   polygon ( INPUT, OUTPUT );
   TYPE
      spantype = 1..30 ;            set the maximum size of
                                    problem as desired
   VAR
      i, j, n : spantype;    area : REAL;
      x, y: ARRAY [ spantype ] OF REAL;

   BEGIN         if your Pascal is interactive, insert:
                    WRITELN ('Number of vertices ?')

   READLN ( n );
   FOR i := 1 TO n DO
      READLN ( x[i], y[i] );     initialize
   area := 0;
   FOR i := 1 TO n DO           e.g. when i=1 then j=2
      BEGIN                          when i=2 then j=3
                                     etc.
         j := ( i MOD n ) + 1;  but when i=n then j=1
         area := area + 0.5*( x[i]*y[j] - x[j]*y[i] )
      END;
   WRITELN ('Area is ', area:8:2 )

   END.
```

Number of vertices?

```
7
0   0
8   6
8   15
3   15
7   12
7   8
0   8
Area is 53.00
```

Two power cables $\vec{a}$ and $\vec{b}$ look uncomfortably close when you superimpose these sketches; what is the shortest distance between $\vec{a}$ & $\vec{b}$?

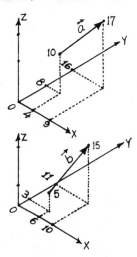

With trigonometry the solution would be messy but with vector algebra it's nice. Express $\vec{a}$ and $\vec{b}$ as vectors:

$$\vec{a} = (9-4)\vec{\imath} + (16-8)\vec{\jmath} + (17-0)\vec{k}$$
$$\vec{b} = (10-6)\vec{\imath} + (11-3)\vec{\jmath} + (15-5)\vec{k}$$

Their cross product, $\vec{a} \times \vec{b}$, is a vector normal to both $\vec{a}$ and $\vec{b}$. Scale this by its own length, $|\vec{a} \times \vec{b}|$, and you have a *unit* vector parallel to $\vec{a} \times \vec{b}$:

$$\vec{u} = \vec{a} \times \vec{b} \div |\vec{a} \times \vec{b}|$$

Take a vector $\vec{c}$ connecting any point on $\vec{a}$ to any point on $\vec{b}$. Here is one of them; it connects the tip of $\vec{a}$ to the tip of $\vec{b}$:

$$\vec{c} = (10-9)\vec{\imath} + (11-16)\vec{\jmath} + (15-17)\vec{k}$$

Distance d, the shortest distance between $\vec{a}$ and $\vec{b}$, is given by the projection of $\vec{c}$ on $\vec{u}$ (the dot product of $\vec{c}$ and $\vec{u}$) which is:

$$d = \vec{c} \cdot \vec{u} \quad \text{which works out at } 3.52 \text{ in this example}$$

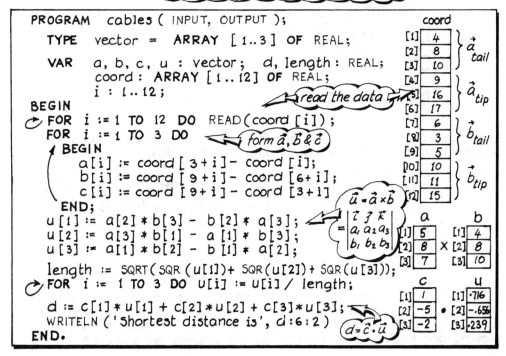

```
PROGRAM   cables ( INPUT, OUTPUT );                            coord
   TYPE   vector =  ARRAY [ 1..3 ] OF REAL;              [1]  4  } a tail
                                                         [2]  8
   VAR    a, b, c, u : vector;   d, length : REAL;       [3] 10
          coord : ARRAY [ 1..12 ] OF REAL;               [4]  9  } a tip
          i : 1..12 ;                  read the data     [5] 16
   BEGIN                                                 [6] 17
     FOR i := 1 TO 12 DO   READ ( coord [i] );           [7]  6  } b tail
     FOR i := 1 TO 3 DO       form a, b & c              [8]  3
      BEGIN                                              [9]  5
         a[i] := coord [ 3+i ] - coord [i];             [10] 10  } b tip
         b[i] := coord [ 9+i ] - coord [6+i];           [11] 11
         c[i] := coord [ 9+i ] - coord [3+i]            [12] 15
      END;
     u [1] := a[2] * b[3] - b[2] * a[3];
     u [2] := a[3] * b[1] - a[1] * b[3];
     u [3] := a[1] * b[2] - b[1] * a[2];
     length := SQRT ( SQR (u[1]) + SQR (u[2]) + SQR (u[3]));
     FOR i := 1 TO 3 DO  u[i] := u[i] / length;

     d := c[1] * u[1] + c[2] * u[2] + c[3] * u[3];
     WRITELN ( 'Shortest distance is', d:6:2 )          d = c · u
   END.
```

$$\vec{u} = \vec{a} \times \vec{b} = \begin{vmatrix} \vec{\imath} & \vec{\jmath} & \vec{k} \\ a_1 & a_2 & a_3 \\ b_1 & b_2 & b_3 \end{vmatrix}$$

a		b
[1] 5	×	[1] 4
[2] 8		[2] 8
[3] 7		[3] 10

c		u
[1] 1		[1] .716
[2] -5	•	[2] -.656
[3] -2		[3] .239

BUBBLE SORT

DAMNED BY ONE OF MY REVIEWERS AS "UNBEATABLE IN ITS INEFFICIENCY"

There are many methods of sorting the contents of an array; a simple technique is the *bubble* or *ripple* sort described below.

To demonstrate the method, take a list of letters. "Index" the first letter and the one following. If the letters indexed are in the right order, leave them alone and advance the index one row. If the letters are in the wrong order, swop them and advance the index one row. Stop one row before the end of the list so as to prevent the second index pointing off the end. Here is the method depicted:

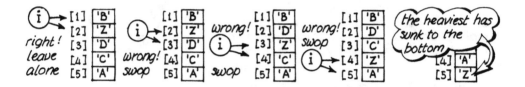

Having sunk the heaviest letter to the bottom it remains to sort the list of letters above it. We set about this precisely as we set about sorting the full list; in other words invoke the same procedure recursively.

The tidiest approach to sorting items is to set up an array of pointers to the items:

[1]	1	→	[1]	'B'
[2]	2	→	[2]	'Z'
[3]	3	→	[3]	'D'
[4]	4	→	[4]	'C'
[5]	5	→	[5]	'A'

pointers   letters

And swop *pointers* rather than the items themselves. When the sorting is finished the arrays should look like this:

e.g. letters[pointers[4]] is 'D'

pointers   letters

This approach holds no particular merit if the aim is only to sort a few letters. But in the real world there might be a lot of information associated with each of the items to be sorted. There is less work in moving one pointer than moving all the information pointed to.

Here is a complete program to sort letters:

```
PROGRAM   bubbles ( INPUT, OUTPUT );

  TYPE   sizetype = 0..30;

  VAR    pointers : ARRAY [ sizetype ] OF sizetype;
         letters : ARRAY [ sizetype ] OF CHAR;
         key: CHAR;   n, i : sizetype;

  PROCEDURE  swop ( VAR p, q : sizetype );

    VAR   tempry : sizetype;

    BEGIN
      tempry := p;   p := q;  q := tempry
    END;

  PROCEDURE   sort ( first, last : sizetype );

    VAR   i : sizetype;   sorted : BOOLEAN;

    BEGIN  { sort }                          SORTING
      IF first < last  THEN                  PROCEDURE
        BEGIN
          sorted := TRUE;
          FOR  i := first  TO last-1  DO
            BEGIN
              IF  letters [pointers[i]] > letters[pointers [i+1]]
                THEN
                  BEGIN
                    swop ( pointers[i], pointers [i+1] );
                    sorted := FALSE              recursive
                  END  { if letters }           invocation
            END;  { for i }
          IF  NOT  sorted  THEN  sort (first, last-1)
        END   { if first < last }
    END;  { sort }

BEGIN   { bubbles }           insert: WRITELN ('Number of letters?')
  READLN ( n );               if your Pascal is interactive
  FOR  i := 1 TO n DO
    BEGIN                          read letters one by one
      READLN (letters[i] );        & set up pointers
      pointers [i] := i
    END;
  sort ( 1, n);          sort them
  WRITELN;
  FOR  i := 1 TO n  DO             display them
    WRITE ( letters [ pointers [i] ] )    in order
END.   { bubbles }
```

```
Number of letters?

5
B
Z
D
C
A

ABCDZ
```

Although the bubble sort is inefficient at sorting a jumbled list, a list in which only one or two items are out of place is sorted very quickly.

QUICKSORT

AN EXAMPLE TO ILLUSTRATE RECURSION AND ANOTHER METHOD OF SORTING

The sorting method called Quicksort was devised by Prof. C.A.R. Hoare. The interpretation below has been formulated to illustrate principles of the method rather than as a practical procedure.

Take some numbers to sort:

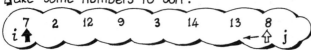

Set pointers i and j at each end of the list as shown. Move j towards i. If j points to a *bigger* number than i does, move j another step towards i.

Now j points to a *smaller* number than i does. So swop the two numbers pointed to, and swop the pointers i and j as well:

Continue moving j towards i ⟨ which now means stepping rightwards instead of leftwards ⟩. If j points to a *smaller* number than i does, move j another step towards i. ⟨ Notice that the *condition* for continuing to move j towards i has been reversed. ⟩

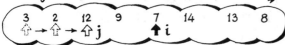

Now j points to a *bigger* number than i does. Swop numbers, pointers, direction and condition exactly as before:

And so on, swopping if necessary ⟨ as already illustrated ⟩ until j meets i:

At which stage it is true to say that every number to the left of i is at least as small as the number pointed to; every number to the right of i is at least as big. In other words the number pointed to has found its resting place. The numbers to the left of i have not, however, been sorted; nor have those to the right of i. But, having described a procedure for locating a resting place which splits a group into two, it remains only to sort the groups to the left and right of i, starting out in each case in the manner already described in detail above.

The logic is depicted below:

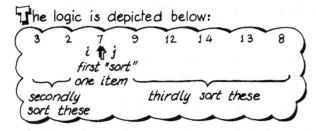

Recursion is applicable when a problem can be reduced to an identical problem ∿ or identical problems ∿ of smaller size. The recursive procedure must, of course, provide the means of escape when the size of problem has been reduced enough. In the case of sorting this should be when the procedure is called upon to sort a single item.

Here is a Quicksort procedure that may be used in place of the bubble sort procedure described on the previous double page:

```
PROCEDURE   sort ( first, last : sizetype );
   VAR
      i, j : sizetype;   jstep : -1..1;   condition: BOOLEAN;
   BEGIN
      IF  first < last          nothing to sort          SUBSTITUTE
         THEN                    unless  first < last     THIS PROCEDURE
            BEGIN                                          IN THE PROGRAM
              i := first;   j := last;                     ON THE PREVIOUS
              jstep := -1;                                 DOUBLE PAGE
              condition := TRUE ;
              REPEAT
                IF condition = ( letters [pointers [i]] > letters [pointers [j]] )
                   THEN                          effectively swop items
                      BEGIN
                        swop ( pointers [i], pointers [j] );
                        swop ( i, j );           swop pointers
                        jstep := - jstep;        reverse direction
                        condition := NOT condition    reverse
                      END;                                 condition
                j := j + jstep
              UNTIL  j = i ;
              sort ( first, i-1 );    recursive
              sort ( i+1 , last )     invocations
            END    { if first < last }    escape if nothing
      END;   { sort }                        to sort
```

Notice how the condition is switched between <= and >. The logical expression: (letters [pointers [i] <= letters [pointers] j]]) takes the value *true* or *false*. This value is compared with the Boolean value stored in the variable named *condition* which is made alternately *true* and *false* by NOT.

Every time the procedure invokes itself the computer has to store away values of its parameters and local variables for possible re-use on return as illustrated by a simpler example of recursion on page 65. In the above example it would be possible to make *jstep* and *condition* global, and so save storage space. But with problems the size of those illustrated in this book it would be silly to do so.

PACKING

A *Boolean value* needs only a single bit (*i.e.* binary digit) for representation ▯; a *character* typically requires four bits ▭; an *integer* 16 or 32 bits ▭. But the unit of storage in a computer is its *word*. The size of this word is dependent on the make and model of computer, 32 bits being typical. It follows that storing Boolean values and characters (perhaps even integers) one per word is wasteful of space.

In Pascal the word PACKED in the definition of an array (or record) gives the compiler permission to pack information more tightly than one item per word. For example:

PACKED ARRAY [1 .. 32768] OF BOOLEAN

might result in the compiler packing the components of this array thirty-two to the word, making something feasible that would otherwise be infeasible. (Some modern compilers pack automatically.)

The price to be paid for saving space is slower retrieval during execution.

Space and speed on some systems may be balanced by packing selectively; say by working on an unpacked array, then copying its contents into a packed array for storage. Procedures PACK and UNPACK are provided by Pascal for such purposes.

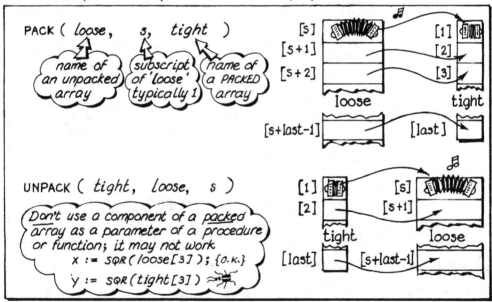

PACK (*loose*, s, *tight*)

name of an unpacked array / *subscript of 'loose' typically 1* / *name of a PACKED array*

[s] [s+1] [s+2] ... [s+last-1]   loose

[1] [2] [3] ... [last]   tight

UNPACK (*tight*, *loose*, s)

Don't use a component of a packed array as a parameter of a procedure or function; it may not work.
x := SQR (loose[3]); {o.k.}
y := SQR (tight[3])

[1] [2] ... [last]   tight

[s] [s+1] ... [s+last-1]   loose

Below are two typical invocations of these standard procedures:

```
VAR  prolix : ARRAY [ 1 .. 1000 ] OF CHAR;
     pith : PACKED ARRAY [ 1 .. 1000 ] OF CHAR;
```

```
PACK ( prolix, 1, pith );
                           UNPACK ( pith, prolix, 1 );
```

INTRODUCING STRINGS

A *string constant* comprises characters enclosed between apostrophes. An apostrophe which is to become part of a string must be written as a pair of apostrophes :

```
WRITELN ( 'Ooh!', 'It''s cold!' )
```
⇨ *Ooh! It's cold!*

For a *string variable* standard Pascal makes do with a PACKED ARRAY [ ] OF CHAR:

```
VAR shiver: PACKED ARRAY [1..10] OF CHAR
```
⇨ shiver ⌊_____⌋
       1   10

String constants may be assigned to string variables :

```
shiver := 'It''s cold!'
WRITELN ( 'Ooh! ',shiver )
```
⇨ *Ooh! It's cold!*

But in standard Pascal the assignment is allowed only if the constant has the same number of characters as the packed array :

```
shiver := 'Ooh!';
shiver := 'Ooh!!!!!';  { O.K.}
```
MANY MODERN PASCAL COMPILERS RELAX THIS RESTRIC-TION OF EQUAL LENGTH

Comparison of strings is allowable provided that the number of characters is the same in each. Any comparator (= , < >, >= *etc.*) may be applied:

```
WRITELN ( shiver = 'Ooh!!!!!' );
WRITELN ( shiver > 'Ooh!');
```
⇨ *TRUE
Error*

The basis of comparison is *ordinal value*. Characters are compared from the left of each string until a mismatch is found. The string in which this mismatching character has the greater ordinal value is considered the greater string. No mismatching character implies the equality of strings :

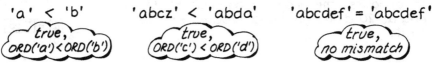

   'a' < 'b'   'abcz' < 'abda'   'abcdef' = 'abcdef'
   true,   *true,*   *true,*
ORD('a')<ORD('b')   *ORD('c')<ORD('d')*   *no mismatch*

Except for the properties of sequences '0' to '9' , 'A' to 'Z' and 'a' to 'z' defined by Pascal the ordinal values of characters depend on the character set on the particular installation; typically ASCII.

Individual characters of a string variable may be manipulated :

```
FOR i := 1 TO 5 DO
   shiver [i + 5] := shiver [i];
WRITELN ( shiver )
```
⇨ *OooohOoooh*

but not all Pascals allow components of *packed* arrays (see opposite) to be used as parameters of procedures: WRITE (shiver [i]), for example, might have to be recast as: ch := shiver[i]; WRITE (ch).

These facilities, although limited, are enough for constructing a set of powerful string-handling procedures as demonstrated in chapter 13.

PARLOUR TRICK

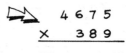

$$4675$$
$$\times \quad 389$$

Amaze your friends. Write down a long multiplication such as this; then start writing down the answer, digit by digit, from right to left, carrying all the working in a cool head.

The trick is mentally to reverse the bottom number, mentally shunting it leftwards past the top number. At each shunt multiply only the digits lying beneath one another, summing the products. Write down the last digit of this sum and carry the rest into the next shunt. The entire process is depicted down the right of the page.

To see how it works, consider each number as a polynomial in 10. In every shunted position the products of terms lying one above the other yield the same power of 10. Furthermore these terms are the *only* terms in the same power of 10 (but not forgetting the carry from above).

$$4 \times 10^3 + 6 \times 10^2 + 7 \times 10^1 + 5 \times 10^0$$
$$9 \times 10^0 + 8 \times 10^1 + 3 \times 10^2$$
$$54 \times 10^2 + 56 \times 10^2 + 15 \times 10^2$$

e.g. all the terms in 10^2

The program opposite automates the method of multiplication described above. It can cope with any reasonable length of multiplication by adjusting the constants *termlimit* and *prodlimit*. As set opposite, the program can multiply terms as long as 20 digits giving a product as long as 40 digits.

To use the program type two terms separated by an asterisk and terminated by an equals sign. Then press [RETURN] .

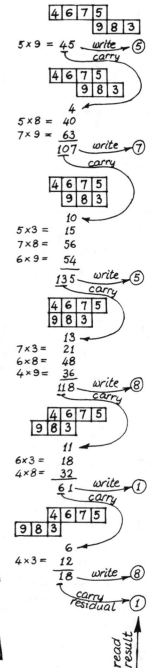

$5 \times 9 = 45$ *write* ⑤   *carry*

$$\begin{aligned}5 \times 8 &= 40\\ 7 \times 9 &= 63\\ \hline 107 \end{aligned}$$ *write* ⑦ *carry*

$$\begin{aligned}5 \times 3 &= 15\\ 7 \times 8 &= 56\\ 6 \times 9 &= 54\\ \hline 135 \end{aligned}$$ *write* ⑤ *carry*

$$\begin{aligned}7 \times 3 &= 21\\ 6 \times 8 &= 48\\ 4 \times 9 &= 36\\ \hline 118 \end{aligned}$$ *write* ⑧ *carry*

$$\begin{aligned}6 \times 3 &= 18\\ 4 \times 8 &= 32\\ \hline 61 \end{aligned}$$ *write* ① *carry*

$$\begin{aligned}4 \times 3 &= 12\\ \hline 18 \end{aligned}$$ *write* ⑧ *carry residual* ①

read result

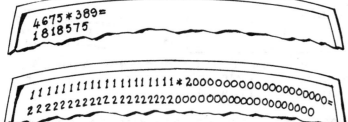

```
4675*389=
1818575
```

```
11111111111111111111*20000000000000000000=
2222222222222222222200000000000000000000
```

```
PROGRAM    parlour ( INPUT, OUTPUT );

  CONST
    termlimit = 2Ø;    prodlimit = 4Ø;

  TYPE
    termspan  =  Ø.. termlimit;
    prodspan  =  Ø.. prodlimit;
    termtype  =  PACKED ARRAY [termspan] OF CHAR;
    prodtype  =  PACKED ARRAY [prodspan] OF CHAR;

  VAR
    a, b : termtype;  c: prodtype; sum, offset: INTEGER;
    na, nb: termspan;  i, k : prodspan;

  PROCEDURE   backhand (VAR x: termtype; VAR count: termspan);

    VAR
      i : INTEGER;  buffer: termtype;

    BEGIN
      i := Ø;
      REPEAT
        READ ( buffer [i] );
        i := SUCC ( i )
      UNTIL  ( buffer [i-1] = '*' )
         OR  ( buffer [i-1] = '=' );
      count := i-2;
      FOR i := Ø TO count DO
        x [i]  := buffer [ count -i]

    END;   { backhand }
```

'backhand' does 3 things
(i) reads a term into a buffer:

4	6	7	5	*
Ø	1	2	3	4

↖count

(ii) counts digits from Ø

(iii) reverses digits into x[ ]

4	6	7	5
3	2	1	Ø

```
BEGIN   { parlour }

  backhand ( a, na);
  backhand ( b, nb);
  sum  := Ø;
  offset := ORD('Ø');

  FOR  k:= Ø TO  na+nb DO
    BEGIN
      FOR i := Ø TO k DO
        IF ( i <= na) AND ( (k-i) <= nb)
          THEN
            sum := sum + (ORD(a[i])-offset)*(ORD(b[k-i])-offset);
        c [k] := CHR ( sum MOD 1Ø + offset );
        sum := sum DIV 1Ø
    END;

  c [ na+ nb+1] :=  CHR ( sum + offset );
  IF sum = Ø THEN i := na+nb ELSE i := na+nb+1;
  FOR k := i DOWNTO Ø DO
    WRITE ( c [k]);
  WRITELN

END.   { parlour }
```

"shunts" as explained opposite

```
           3  2  1  Ø
a →   | 4 | 6 | 7 | 5 |
              | 9 | 8 | 3 | ←b
                0   1   2
```
↖na ↘nb

residual carry

but suppress any leading zero

A decimal (base 10) number is a polynomial in ten as emphasized on the previous page. Similarly a *hex* number (base 16) is a polynomial in sixteen, an *octal* number (base 8) a polynomial in eight, and so on. In general, a number to base *b* is a polynomial in *b* and *b* digits are required to express it. For digits bigger than 9, capital letters are pressed into service; letters A to V cope with bases up to base 32.

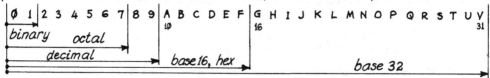

In the following program characters 'Ø' to 'V' are held as a string constant (*refconst*) which is assigned to a packed array of characters named *refstring*. This array is used in two ways. Given a character representing a digit (say a *hex* digit) the corresponding numerical value may be found by matching the digit against each character in turn, the array subscript indicating ordinal value when a match is found. Conversely, by using the ordinal value as an array subscript the corresponding character may be picked out without need of a search.

The above principles are employed in procedures *find* and *outdigit* respectively. Unfortunately some Pascals forbid assignment of a string constant to an array of the type:

PACKED ARRAY [Ø..31] OF CHAR

insisting that the lower bound be always unity, *e.g.* [1..32]. The array subscript therefore cannot express ordinal value directly but has to be offset by 1. Not nice.

The program is designed to read a number expressed relative to one base and write the same number expressed to another base. For example if the program were given:

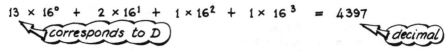
112D   16   8
(original number)   (existing base)   (desired base)

it would convert the 112D from *hex* to *octal* and display 10455.

The program first looks up the ordinal values of digits D, 2, 1, 1 and evaluates a polynomial in 16 :

$$13 \times 16^0 + 2 \times 16^1 + 1 \times 16^2 + 1 \times 16^3 = 4397$$

(corresponds to D)   (decimal)

The looking up is done by procedure *find* and the polynomial is evaluated by procedure *decimal*. Notice that *find* returns −1 if unable to find a match within the range of the current base. If *decimal* receives −1 from *find* it returns a zero result to the main program.

```pascal
PROGRAM  bases( INPUT, OUTPUT );
  CONST
    stringlength = 32;
    refconst = '0123456789ABCDEFGHIJKLMNOPQRSTUV';
```

'refconst' is assigned to 'refstring' in the main program

```pascal
  TYPE
    stringrange = 1.. stringlength;
    stringtype = PACKED ARRAY [ stringrange] OF CHAR;
    basetype = 2..32;
    number = 0.. MAXINT;
  VAR
    instring, outstring, refstring :  stringtype;
    inlength, outlength :  stringrange;
    ch: CHAR;   dec, i : number;
    basenow, baserequired : basetype;
```

```pascal
  FUNCTION  find( ch: CHAR;  base: basetype ): INTEGER;
    VAR
       found: BOOLEAN;   i: number;
    BEGIN
      i := 1;
      REPEAT
        found := ( ch= refstring[i] );
        IF NOT found THEN i:= SUCC(i)
      UNTIL found OR ( i > base );
      IF found
        THEN  find := i-1
        ELSE  find := -1
    END;
```

do not search beyond range of given base

```pascal
  FUNCTION  decimal (string: stringtype; length: stringrange;
                     base: basetype ) : INTEGER;
    VAR
       digit, power : INTEGER;  n: number;
       i: stringrange; silly: BOOLEAN;
    BEGIN
      n := 0;  silly := FALSE;  power := 1;
      FOR  i := length DOWNTO 1 DO
        BEGIN
          digit := find ( string[i], base );
          IF  digit < 0
            THEN
              silly := TRUE
            ELSE
              BEGIN
                n := n + digit * power;
                power := power * base
              END
        END;
      IF silly  THEN decimal := 0
                ELSE decimal := n
    END;
```

e.g. if base = 16 then 'power' goes 1, 16, 16^2, 16^3...

continued overleaf

To convert the intermediate decimal value to a number expressed to a new base the program keeps dividing by the new base, taking note of the remainders. The remainders are the ordinal values of the result in reverse order.

```
8) 4397
   8) 549    rem  5
      8) 68   rem  5
         8) 8  rem  4
            8) 1 rem  0
               0 rem  1
```

The ordinal values 10455 are looked up in the array of characters to give the digits of the result. These are 10455 ≈ apparently not worth "looking up". But if the required base were to be 32 the ordinal values would be 4, 9, 13. Looking these up in the array would give 49D.

```
32) 4397
    32) 137   rem  13
        32) 4  rem  9
            0   rem  4
```

Conversion to the required base is performed by procedure *outdigit*. Recursion is used to solve the problem of digits being computed in reverse order.

```
PROCEDURE  outdigit (n:number; base: basetype);

VAR
   m : number;  c: CHAR;
BEGIN

   m :=  n DIV base;
   c :=  refstring [1 + (n MOD base)] ;
   IF  m <> 0
      THEN
         outdigit ( m, base);
   WRITE ( c )

END;
```

"look up" digit
e.g. 8 gives 8
      13 gives D

recursion to write digits in reverse order

```
BEGIN   { PROGRAM }

   refstring := refconst;
   i := 1;
   REPEAT
      READ ( ch);
      instring[i]  := ch;
      i := SUCC(i)
   UNTIL   ch = ' ';
   inlength := i - 2;
   READLN ( basenow, baserequired);
   dec := decimal ( instring, inlength, basenow);
   outdigit ( dec, baserequired);
   WRITELN

END.
```

INPUT

112D 16 8
10455

OUTPUT

10455 8 16
112D

There are three sales people selling four products. Quantities sold are tabulated in table A. ▷

A

	PRODUCT			
SALES PERSON	1]	2]	3]	4]
[1,	5	2	0	10
[2,	3	5	2	5
[3,	20	0	0	0

B

PRODUCT	1]	2]
[1,	1.50	0.20
[2,	2.80	0.40
[3,	5.00	1.00
[4,	2.00	0.50

PRICE COMMISSION

◁ Table B shows the price of each product and the commission earned for selling each item.

The money brought in is calculated as follows:

SALES PERSON
$$[1 \quad 5*1.50 + 2*2.80 + 0*5.00 + 10*2.00 = 33.10$$
$$[2 \quad 3*1.50 + 5*2.80 + 2*5.00 + 5*2.00 = 38.50$$
$$[3 \quad 20*1.50 + 0*2.80 + 0*5.00 + 0*2.00 = 30.00$$

And the commissions earned as follows:

SALES PERSON
$$[1 \quad 5*0.20 + 2*0.40 + 0*1.00 + 10*0.50 = 6.80$$
$$[2 \quad 3*0.20 + 5*0.40 + 2*1.00 + 5*0.50 = 7.10$$
$$[3 \quad 20*0.20 + 0*0.40 + 0*1.00 + 0*0.50 = 4.00$$

This computation is called *matrix multiplication* and looks best set out thus:▷

$$
A\begin{matrix}[1,\\[2,\\[3,\end{matrix}
\begin{bmatrix} 5 & 2 & 0 & 10 \\ 3 & 5 & 2 & 5 \\ 20 & 0 & 0 & 0 \end{bmatrix}
\; * \;
B\begin{matrix}[1,\\[2,\\[3,\\[4,\end{matrix}
\begin{bmatrix} 1.50 & 0.20 \\ 2.80 & 0.40 \\ 5.00 & 1.00 \\ 2.00 & 0.50 \end{bmatrix}
\; = \;
C\begin{matrix}[1,\\[2,\\[3,\end{matrix}
\begin{bmatrix} 33.10 & 6.80 \\ 38.50 & 7.10 \\ 30.00 & 4.00 \end{bmatrix}
$$

(the number of __columns__ of A must be the same as) .... *(the number of __rows__ of B)* °°°° *(and the result has as many __rows__ as A & as many __columns__ as B)*

Here is a program to input data for matrices A & B, multiply them together, then display their product, matrix c:

```
PROGRAM    sales ( INPUT, OUTPUT );
   TYPE
      atype = ARRAY [ 1..3, 1..4 ] OF INTEGER;
      btype = ARRAY [ 1..4, 1..2 ] OF REAL;
      ctype = ARRAY [ 1..3, 1..2 ] OF REAL;
   VAR
      a: atype; b: btype;  c: ctype; n,i,j,k: INTEGER;
BEGIN
   FOR n := 1 TO 3 DO
      READLN ( a[n,1], a[n,2], a[n,3], a[n,4] );
   FOR n := 1 TO 4 DO
      READLN ( b[n,1], b[n,2] );
   FOR i := 1 TO 2 DO
      FOR j := 1 TO 3 DO
        BEGIN
           c[i,j] := 0;
           FOR k := 1 TO 4 DO
             c[j,i] := c[j,i] + a[j,k] * b[k,i];
        END;
   FOR n := 1 TO 3 DO WRITELN ( c[n,1]:8:2, c[n,2]:8:2 )
END.
```

try this with the values in A & B above

CONFORMANT ARRAY PARAMETERS *DEEP BREATH IN...*

The program on the previous page could be recast by parcelling the matrix multiplication as a procedure:

```
PROCEDURE  matmul (VAR p: atype; VAR q: btype; VAR r: ctype);
  VAR
    i, j, k : INTEGER;
  BEGIN
    FOR i := 1 TO 2 DO
      FOR j := 1 TO 3  DO
        BEGIN
          r [j, i] := 0;
          FOR k := 1  TO  4 DO
            r [j, i] := r [j, i] + p [j, k] * q [k, i]
        END
  END;
```

although p&q are not altered by this procedure, parameters which are names of arrays should always be VAR parameters; otherwise the program has to take copies of the arrays on each invocation. NB!

The main program then simplifies to:

```
BEGIN   { PROGRAM }
  FOR n := 1 TO  3   DO
    READLN ( a[n,1], a[n,2], a [n, 3], a [n, 4] );
  FOR n := 1 TO 4  DO
    READLN ( b[n,1], b[n,2] );
  matmul ( a, b, c );

  FOR n := 1 TO 3  DO WRITELN ( c[n,1]:8:2, c[n,2]:8:2 )
END.
```

invoke the procedure for arrays a, b, c

This is fine provided that the ranges of i, j and k in the FOR loops of *matmul* conform to the dimensions of arrays of *atype*, *btype* and *ctype* as declared in the TYPE section of the main program:

```
TYPE
  atype = ARRAY [ 1..3,  1..4 ] OF  INTEGER;
  btype = ARRAY [ 1..4,  1..2 ] OF  REAL;
  ctype = ARRAY [ 1..3,  1..2 ] OF REAL
```

But if circumstances made the programmer expand the dimensions of these array-types then the programmer would have to change the ranges of i, j, k in the FOR loops of *matmul*, making them conform to the new dimensions.   A potential source of trouble.

A partial solution to the problem has been specified in Pascal to BS6192. When using arrays as parameters (such as p, q, r in *matmul*) the idea is to declare them as *conformant arrays*. A conformant array is one that *conforms* in dimensionality and in its type of component with the type of of an array declared in an outer block ≈ typically in the TYPE section of the main program.   The programmer tells the Pascal compiler that an array is *conformant* by specifying *conformant array parameters*. At the top of the opposite page is the *matmul* procedure rewritten so as to contain conformant array parameters.

```
PROCEDURE  matmul( VAR p: ARRAY [1..rp: INTEGER; 1..cp: INTEGER ] OF  INTEGER;
                   VAR q: ARRAY [1..cp: INTEGER; 1..cq: INTEGER] OF REAL;
                   VAR r: ARRAY [1..rp: INTEGER; 1..cq: INTEGER] OF REAL);
   VAR i, j, k: INTEGER;
   BEGIN
     FOR  i := 1 TO  cq  DO
       FOR  j := 1 TO  rp  DO
         BEGIN
           r[j, i]:= 0;
           FOR k := 1 TO cp DO
             r[j, i] := r[j, i] + p[j, k] * q[k, i]
         END
   END;
```

this is a conformant array parameter; r is the conformant array which must "conform" in dimensionality and component-type and state of packing with any array nominated as an actual parameter

The invocation of *matmul* remains exactly as before:

```
matmul ( a, b, c );
```

So how is *matmul* to know the values for *cq*, *rp* and *cp*? That is the clever bit. Conformant array parameters provide enough information for *matmul* to peep at the declarations of these arrays in the invoking program. Here it is pictorially for array *p* when the program invokes *matmul* with actual parameter *a* :

in the invoking program

in the procedure definition

```
matmul( a, b,c );    VAR a: atype;    atype = ARRAY [1..3
matmul ( p: ARRAY [1..rp : INTEGER
```

Provided that arrays *p* and *a* are conformant (both two-dimensional; both with components of type INTEGER; both unpacked) each name such as *rp* becomes associated with a dimension such as *3*.

Conformant array parameters do *not* provide dynamic array bounds, only the ability to pick up automatically the fixed dimensions declared in the original TYPE declaration. A complicated facility for achieving little. Few Pascals provide conformant array parameters.

Dynamic array bounds of limited scope may be simulated by declaring oversized arrays and making parameters of the current dimensions. The following fragments of program should convey the idea:

```
TYPE   atype =  ARRAY [ 1..20, 1..20 ];     oversized declarations
```

```
PROCEDURE matmul (p: atype; q: btype; r: ctype; i, j, k: INTEGER );
```

```
matmul ( a, b, c, 2, 3, 4 );     invocation       dimensions as parameters
```

Conformant array parameters would enable *matmul* to tell only that the maximum allowable dimensions were 20.   *BREATHE... OUT!*

EXERCISES

1. Implement *bubbles* with the constant named *sizetype* set to a more challenging size than 30 — say 100 or 150. Then take some timings:

- when the input sequence is made random by stabbing at the keyboard without trying to make a pattern

- when the input sequence is generally sorted:

  AAAA BB CCCCCC DDE ...

  but with the occasional letter out of sequence:

  ... E Z FFF GGGG ...

2. Repeat the exercise using Quicksort (page 87) in place of bubble sort (page 85). What conclusions do you draw from the results?

3. Using program *bases* as a model, develop specific procedures for:

- converting from *hex* to *decimal*
- converting from *decimal* to *hex*

By removing the generality from *bases* you should end up with two short, elegant and useful procedures.

4. If you are familiar with matrix algebra develop a set of procedures like *matmul* for addition, transposition and (a challenge) inversion. Use parameters for current dimensions as described at the bottom of the previous page.

RECORDS

INTRODUCING RECORDS

Whereas an *array* is an arrangement of components of identical type, a *record* is an arrangement of components generally of *different* type. Compare the following type of array: ➪

```
TYPE
    nametype = PACKED ARRAY [1..10] OF CHAR;
    infotype = ARRAY [1..3] OF nametype;
```

"infotype"

[1] \
[2] \
[3]

an array of packed arrays

with this type of *record*: ➪

```
TYPE
    nametype = PACKED ARRAY [1..10] OF CHAR;
    detailtype =
      RECORD
        surname, forename: nametype;
        age: 18..65;
        grade: (jr, sr, exec)
      END
```

"detailtype"

•surname \
•forename \
•age ☐ \
•grade ☐

a record having various types of field

Just as variables may be whole arrays:

```
VAR
    a, b: infotype;
```

a[1] \
a[2] \
a[3] \
variable a

b[1] \
b[2] \
b[3] \
variable b

so may variables be whole *records*:

```
VAR
    q, r: detailtype;
```

q.surname \
q.forename \
q.age ☐ \
q.grade ☐ \
variable q

r.surname \
r.forename \
r.age ☐ \
r.grade ☐ \
variable r

Much as components of arrays are addressed by *subscripts* (in square brackets):

```
a[i] := 'Wilberforc';    b[2] := a[i];
```

a[i] Wilberforc \
b[2] Wilberforc

the components of records are addressed by *field name* (after a full stop):

```
q.surname := 'Wilberforc';
q.age := 22; q.grade := jr;
r.forename := q.surname;
```

q.surname Wilberforc \
q.age 22   q.grade jr \
r.forename Wilberforc

The sketches illustrate records which have components of various types including packed arrays. Conversely, the components of an array may be *records*. The only restriction to the mixture of types in arrays and records concerns *arrays*: in any *one* array *all* components must be of the same type. An example of an array of records is:

```
VAR  people: ARRAY [1..100] OF detailtype
```

'people' is now an array of 100 personnel records

SYNTAX OF RECORDS

The syntax of record type (excluding *variants* which are explained later) is:

The syntax for referring to a component of a record is:

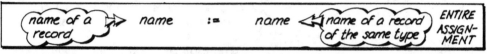

Whereas arrays are manipulated by means of *subscripts*, records are manipulated by means of *field names* which are analogous to subscripts. But there is an important exception; a copy of the *entire* content of one record may be assigned to another *of the same type* in a single operation:

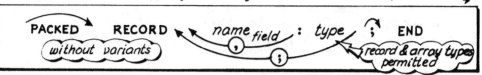

where "same type" means a type with the *same name*; a type with the same specification is not enough. A similar requirement applying to the entire assignment of arrays is illustrated on page 81.

The word PACKED in front of RECORD implies the same thing as it does in front of ARRAY. A packed record occupies less space than the corresponding unpacked record at the cost of slower retrieval during execution. The procedures PACK and UNPACK (page 88) are not applicable to records; only to arrays.

In any one type of record ≈ including all records that may be nested within it ≈ every field name must be unique. Field names in different types of record, however, may be identical without causing interference:

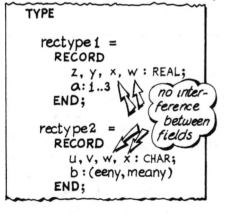

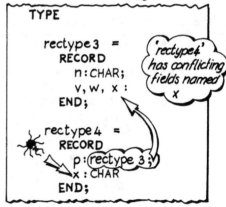

PERSONNEL RECORDS

AN EXAMPLE ILLUSTRATING THE USE OF RECORDS

This program prompts for an employee's surname, forename, age and executive grade. Terminate every answer by pressing the RETURN key. When there are no more records the program sorts all given records by each of four sorting keys :

- surname 〔 alphabetical order 〕
- forename 〔 alphabetical order 〕
- age 〔 ascending numerical order 〕
- grade 〔ascending ordinal value: JR, SR, EXEC〕

```
More? (Y/N): Y
Surname?(<=10chars):HAIG
Forename?(<=10chars):JOHN
Age?(18to65):40
Grade?(JR,SR,EXEC):EXEC

More? (Y/N): Y
Surname?(<=10chars):DAVIS
Forename?(<=10chars):SAMUEL
Age?(18to65): 64
Grade? (JR,SR,EXEC):JR
More? (Y/N): N
```
INPUT

OUTPUT

```
DAVIS   SAMUEL  64  Junior
HAIG    JOHN    40  Executive    by surname
****
HAIG    JOHN    40  Executive    by forename
DAVIS   SAMUEL  64  Junior
****
HAIG    JOHN    40  Executive    by age
DAVIS   SAMUEL  64  Junior
****
DAVIS   SAMUEL  64  Junior       by grade
HAIG    JOHN    40  Executive
```

There are minimal checks on data . A grade other than JR, SR or EXEC is treated as JR by default; a response to *More?* other than Y implies N; other errors 〔 such as a name longer than 10 letters 〕 are trapped by the Pascal processor.

The example shown here assumes a Pascal processor that can be used interactively. Chapter 11 describes some of the potential hiccups caused by interactive input.

The allowable length of name and allowable number of records are set into constants for ease of adjustment. The type of personnel record is that already illustrated and depicted again below. Associated with its fields 〔 *surname, forename, age* and *grade* 〕 are elements of an enumerated *keytype* 〔 *lastname, firstname, decrepitude* and *clout* 〕. This is used in the sorting procedure for locating the appropriate sorting key. The personnel records are stored in array *a*; associated pointers are stored in array *p*. The pointers are used for sorting as explained on page 84.

Here are the declarations:

```
PROGRAM   personnel ( INPUT, OUTPUT );

CONST   namelength = 10; listlength = 30; space = ' ';

TYPE  nametype = PACKED ARRAY [1..namelength] OF CHAR;
      detailtype =
        RECORD
          surname, forename: nametype;
          age: 18..65;
          grade: (jr, sr, exec)
        END
      indextype = 0..listlength;
      keytype = (lastname, firstname, decrepitude, clout);
      ordertype = (gt, eq);
```

· surname
· forename
· age
· grade
detailtype

```
VAR  a: ARRAY [indextype] OF detailtype;      ← array of personnel records
     p: ARRAY [indextype] OF indextype;       ← pointers for sorting
     key: keytype;                            ← sorting key
     count : indextype;                       ← count of records
```

The main program is shown overleaf. The main program (A) invokes the input procedure (B), then invokes ⇌ four times each ⇌ the sorting procedure (C) and listing procedure (D). The input procedure (B) invokes a special procedure (E) for accepting a string of characters; it also invokes a function (F) for testing the equality of two strings. The sorting procedure (C) also invokes func-

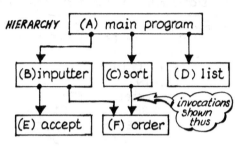

tion (F) to test whether one string is "greater" than another. To avoid using the FORWARD directive these subprograms should be arranged such that (E) and (F) precede (B), that (F) also precedes (C). The main program (A) must come last.

This is the procedure (E) for accepting data from the keyboard:

```
PROCEDURE  accept ( VAR linebuf: nametype);

   VAR  i : 0..namelength;   ch : CHAR;
                                                        ← fill line buffer
   BEGIN                                                   with spaces
↪  FOR  i := 1 TO namelength DO linebuf[i] := space;
↪  REPEAT  READ(linebuf[i]) UNTIL linebuf[i] <> space;
     i := 1;                                        first character      ignore leading
     WHILE NOT EOLN DO                               in linebuf[1]          spaces
       BEGIN
         i := i + 1;                                continue from
         READ ( linebuf [i]);                       linebuf [2]
       END;
     READLN;
   END;
```

Here is the function (F) for comparing strings for equality or relative order :

```
FUNCTION  order ( c: ordertype; a, b: nametype ): BOOLEAN;

   VAR  i : 0..namelength;   c1, c2, null : CHAR;

   BEGIN                                    an invisible character
     i := 0;    null := CHR(0);             with lower ordinal value
     REPEAT            global               than any letter or digit
       i := i + 1;     constant
       IF  a[i] = space THEN c1:= null  ELSE  c1 := a[i];
       IF  b[i] = space THEN c2:= null  ELSE  c2 := b[i];
     UNTIL (( i = namelength) OR (c1<>c2)) OR (( c1=null ) AND (c2=null));
     CASE  c  OF
       gt:    order := ( c1 > c2);
       eq:    order := ( c1 = c2)
     END  { CASE }
   END;
```

PERSONNEL RECORDS (CONTINUED)

The sorting procedure (c) employs the bubble technique explained earlier but adapted to cope with different sorting keys. Each key signifies a different criterion for ordering. Differences are resolved by a CASE statement having a structure similar to that of the personnel record.

```
PROCEDURE  sort ( n: indextype ;  k: keytype );
   VAR    s, sorted: BOOLEAN;    i, tempry: indextype;
   BEGIN
     IF n>1 THEN
       BEGIN
         sorted := TRUE ;
         FOR i := 1 TO n-1 DO           signifies which of the four
           BEGIN                        keys is to be sorted
             CASE k OF
             lastname :
               s := order(gt, a[p[i]].surname, a[p[i+1]].surname );
             firstname :
               s := order(gt, a[p[i]].forename, a[p[i+1]].forename);
             decrepitude:
               s := a[p[i]].age > a[p[i+1]].age;
             clout:
               s := ORD(a[p[i]].grade) > ORD(a[p[i+1]].grade)
             END; { CASE }
             IF S THEN            s signifies TRUE or FALSE
               BEGIN
                 sorted := FALSE;
                 tempry := p[i];       swop pointers
                 p[i] := p[i+1];        if TRUE
                 p[i+1] := tempry
               END                      recursive
           END; { FOR i }              invocation
         IF NOT sorted THEN  sort(n-1, k)
       END  { IF n>1 }
   END;
```

alphabetical keys · *numerical key* · *ordinal key*

The listing procedure (D) is straightforward:

```
PROCEDURE  list ( n: indextype );
   VAR  i: indextype;
   BEGIN
     FOR i := 1 TO n DO
       BEGIN  { FOR i}
         WRITE ( a[p[i]]. surname , space);
         WRITE ( a[p[i]].forename , space);
         WRITE ( a[p[i]].age:3,   space );
         CASE  a[p[i]].grade  OF
           jr: WRITELN ('Junior');
           sr: WRITELN ('Senior');
           exec: WRITELN ('Executive')
         END  { CASE }
       END { FOR i }
   END;
```

].surname `CANDLEWICK`
].forename `JOSIAH`
].age `19`   *EXAMPLE*
].grade `jr`

remember you cannot WRITE a component of enumerated type; hence the CASE statement

Despite a lamentable lack of checks, the input procedure (B) is the most tedious to write. Input procedures in any language become so.

If your program gets the hiccups, asking for data it has already been given (see chapter 11), the remedy is to remove all the prompts and set up a file of input data. Consult your local manual about typing, editing and saving an input file to be read by a Pascal program.

```
PROCEDURE  inputter ( VAR n: indextype );

  VAR indicator: CHAR;                    ⟸  indicator Y for Yes
      string: nametype;                   ⟸  string ░░░░░░░░░
      buffer: detailtype;
                                              buffer.surname ░░░░░░░░░░
  BEGIN                                       buffer.forename ░░░░░░░░░░
    n := 0;                                   buffer.age  ░░░   18..65
    REPEAT                                    buffer.grade ░░░  (JR,SR,EXEC)
      WRITE ('More? (Y/N): ');
      READLN ( indicator );            p[1] 1 →
      IF  indicator = 'Y'              p[2] 2 →
        THEN                           p[3] 3 →
          BEGIN                        p[4] 4 →
            n := n + 1;
            p[n] := n;
            WRITE ('Surname? (<= 10 chars) : ');
            accept ( string); buffer. surname := string;
            WRITE ('Forename? (<= 10 chars) : ');
            accept ( string); buffer. forename := string;
            WRITE ('Age? (18 to 65) : ' );
            READLN ( buffer. age );
            WRITE ('Grade? (JR, SR, EXEC) : ');
            buffer. grade := jr;
            accept ( string);
            IF order (eq, string, 'EXEC      ') THEN buffer.grade:= exec;
            IF order (eq, string, 'SR        ') THEN buffer.grade:= sr;
            a[n] := buffer         entire assignment of record
          END                         'buffer' to component 'a[n]'
        ELSE
          IF  indicator = 'N' THEN WRITELN ('Normal ending')
                              ELSE WRITELN ('Abnormal ending');
    UNTIL  indicator <> 'Y';
  END;  {inputter}
```

The main program (A) is simple:

```
BEGIN
  inputter ( count );                           MAIN
                                                PROGRAM
  FOR key := lastname TO  clout  DO
    BEGIN
      sort (count, key);            the sorting key
      list ( count);                cycles all four
      WRITELN (' **** ')            fields of the
    END                             record
END.  {PROGRAM}
```

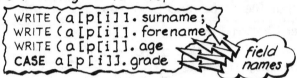

Notice the repetition of a[p[i]]. *(full stop)* in the listing procedure on page 104. The thing that most distinguishes one line from the next is the field-name following the full stop.

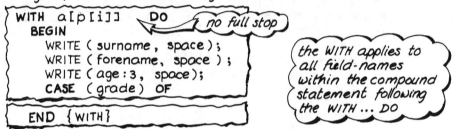

```
WRITE ( a [ p [ i ] ] . surname ;
WRITE ( a [ p [ i ] ] . forename
WRITE ( a [ p [ i ] ] . age
CASE a [ p [ i ] ] . grade
```

field names

The WITH statement is designed to supply a single specified record name (as far as the full stop) so that statements such as those shown above may be reduced to their distinguishing features. Here are the statements again, but in full and using WITH.

```
WITH  a [ p [ i ] ]       DO        no full stop
   BEGIN
      WRITE ( surname , space );
      WRITE ( forename , space ) ;
      WRITE ( age : 3 , space );
      CASE ( grade ) OF

   END { WITH }
```

the WITH applies to all field-names within the compound statement following the WITH ... DO

The syntax of the WITH statement is:

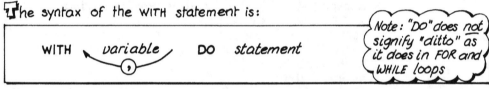

WITH ‚ *variable* ‚ DO *statement*

Note: "DO" does not signify "ditto" as it does in FOR and WHILE loops

where:

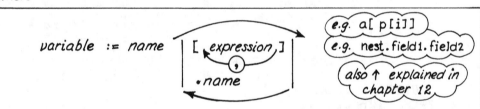

variable := *name* [*expression*] / .*name*

e.g. a[p[i]]

e.g. nest.field1.field2

also ↑ explained in chapter 12

The declarations below are needed by the programs opposite which demonstrate the implications of a WITH statement in the context of a nested record:

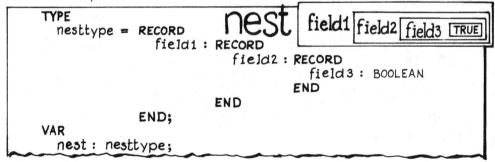

```
TYPE                        nest   field1 field2 field3 TRUE
   nesttype = RECORD
                   field1 : RECORD
                              field2 : RECORD
                                         field3 : BOOLEAN
                                       END
                            END
              END;
VAR
   nest : nesttype;
```

The first demonstration below shows that the WITH statement may be made to reach any level of nesting (does a nest have "levels"? "Layers" would mix the metaphor less but "levels" is the accepted term):

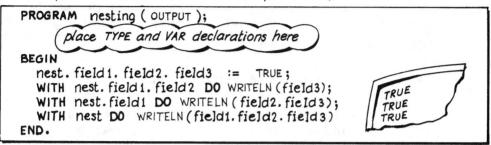

```
PROGRAM  nesting ( OUTPUT );
     place TYPE and VAR declarations here
BEGIN
   nest. field1. field2. field3  :=   TRUE ;
   WITH  nest. field1. field2 DO WRITELN (field3);
   WITH  nest. field1 DO  WRITELN ( field2. field3);
   WITH  nest DO  WRITELN (field1. field2. field3)
END.
```
```
TRUE
TRUE
TRUE
```

The next demonstration illustrates nested WITH statements reflecting the structure of the nested record:

```
PROGRAM   nesting2( OUTPUT );
     place TYPE and VAR declarations here
BEGIN
   nest. field1. field2.field3  :=   TRUE;
   WITH   nest DO
     WITH  field1  DO
       WITH  field2  DO
          WRITELN ( field3)
END.
```
```
TRUE
```

The third demonstration is to illustrate the implication of using commas in place of full stops. This syntax appears to imply the option of nominating more than one type of record. But this would be impossible because

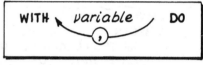

WITH ← variable , DO

the compiler could not then know to which record each field-name belonged (recall that several records may use the same name for distinct fields). The commas are no more than alternatives to full stops. Compare the following program with the program at the top of this page.

```
PROGRAM   nesting3 ( OUTPUT );
     place TYPE and VAR declarations here
BEGIN
   nest. field1. field2. field3 :=   TRUE;
   WITH   nest, field1, field2 DO WRITELN ( field3);
   WITH   nest, field1 DO  WRITELN( field2. field3);
   WITH   nest DO  WRITELN(field1. field2. field3)
END.
```
```
TRUE
TRUE
TRUE
```

The comma notation works only after WITH; do not try:

      WITH   nest DO WRITELN (field1, field2, field3);

and do not permute:

      WITH   field2, nest, field1 DO WRITELN (field3);

Consider a program for managing a car-sharing scheme devised to soften the impact of a bus or rail strike. The following record might occur:

```
PROGRAM   carshare ( INPUT, OUTPUT );
   TYPE
      modetype = ( foot, pushbike, motorbike, car );

      gotype =  RECORD
                  surname: PACKED ARRAY [ 1..10 ] OF CHAR;
                  initial: CHAR;
                  mode: modetype;
                  year: 1900..1990;
                  sidecar: BOOLEAN;
                  mpg: REAL;
                  seats: 1..6
               END;
   VAR
      person: gotype;  people: ARRAY [ 1..100 ] OF gotype;
      i: 1..100;
```

This record must be filled in carefully because not all fields are relevant to every case; a pedestrian, for example, has no mpg or seats. It is the item in the *mode* field that determines which subsequent fields are relevant to each case. So a CASE statement is appropriate to filling in or printing records. For example:

```
WITH  people [ i ]  DO
   BEGIN
      WRITELN ( initial, surname : 11 );
      CASE  mode  OF
         foot, pushbike : ;          null statement
         motorbike: BEGIN   WRITE ('Bike made in ', year);
                       IF  sidecar  THEN  WRITELN (' with room for 1')
                                    ELSE  WRITELN (' pillion only')
                    END; {motorbike}
         car: WRITELN ( year:4, mpg:4:1, ' room for', seats-1:2 )
      END  {CASE mode }
   END; { WITH }
```

this WRITE statement is common to all modes of transport

conventional CASE statement

But there are problems; every record has to have the capacity to store every possible arrangement of data. Space is wasted; in a practical program the wastage could be prodigious. So Pascal provides for a variation in arrangement from record to record like this:

The part of the record which varies in arrangement is called the *variant*. The variant always comes *last*. The field (in this case •*mode*) which discriminates between variants is called the *tag field*.

To specify a variant a special statement is employed. Its name is CASE but this statement is distinct from the *control* statement of the same name. Nevertheless, similarities between the two statements are evident. Here is a new definition of *gotype*:

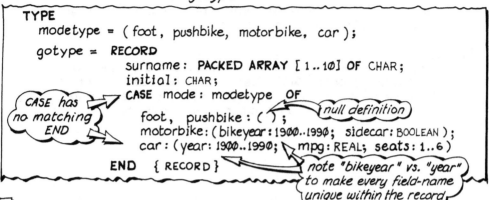

```
TYPE
    modetype = ( foot, pushbike, motorbike, car );

    gotype =  RECORD
                surname: PACKED ARRAY [ 1..10] OF CHAR;
                initial: CHAR;
                CASE mode: modetype  OF
                    foot, pushbike: ( );
                    motorbike: (bikeyear: 1900..1990; sidecar: BOOLEAN );
                    car: (year: 1900..1990; mpg: REAL; seats: 1..6)
            END   { RECORD }
```

CASE has no matching END

null definition

note "bikeyear" vs. "year" to make every field-name unique within the record

The above defines the type of record depicted in all its guises at the foot of the opposite page.

Access to the newly-defined record is no simpler than it was previously; indeed it is more complicated because there are now *different* components for storing the year of manufacture (change WRITE('Bike made in', year) to WRITE('Bike made in', bikeyear) to update the fragment of program opposite). The conventional CASE statement is still needed to protect pedestrians and cyclists from being expected to carry passengers.

The syntax of *variant* is defined recursively as follows:

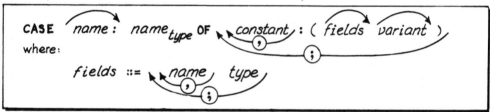

```
CASE  name : name_type OF  constant , : ( fields  variant )
where:                            ,        ;
       fields ::=   name , type
                       ,    ;
```

Notice there is no END to match CASE. Because the variant must come last it is deemed to share its END with the END which matches RECORD.

Notice that (*fields variant*) permits both items to be absent, hence an empty pair of brackets to signify a null definition of *fields* (as used in the example above). Conversely the presence of a *variant* introduces a further CASE, causing variants to become nested. And because *fields* in any variant may be omitted it follows that no restriction on complexity is imposed by the rule that the variant must come last.

Omitting *name:* implies the absence of a tag field to discriminate between variants. Such a record is called a *free union* (as opposed to a *discriminated union* when there is a tag field). A free union allows an item to be stored under the guise of a character, for example, but retrieved as though it were an integer ≈ and similarly for other equivalences of type. A free union designed to peek at pointers (naughty) is given by Grogono along with appropriate warnings about such practice. See bibliography.

EXERCISES

1. Implement the *personnel* program. Improve the program by defining a more realistic record.

2. Write a Quicksort procedure to replace the bubble-sort procedure on page 104. Does it sort the records any faster? (The scale of this exercise is so small that one sorting procedure is as good as another. The simpler the better.)

INTRODUCING FILES
THE MEANS OF COMMUNICATION BETWEEN PROGRAMS

The file named OUTPUT has already been demonstrated. The name OUTPUT is *implied* when omitted from a WRITE (or WRITELN) statement but may be included if desired:

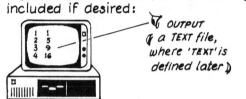

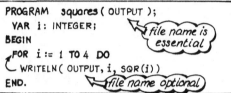
OUTPUT
(a TEXT file, where 'TEXT' is defined later)

```
PROGRAM  squares ( OUTPUT );
  VAR i: INTEGER;              ┌─ file name is
BEGIN                         │    essential
  ┌FOR i := 1 TO 4 DO
  └ WRITELN( OUTPUT, i, SQR(i) )
  END.                   ┌─ file name optional
```

The file named INPUT has also been demonstrated. The name INPUT is *implied* when omitted from a READ, READLN, EOF or EOLN procedure or function but may be included if desired:

INPUT
(a TEXT file)

OUTPUT

```
PROGRAM  anysquares (INPUT, OUTPUT);
  VAR i,j,k : INTEGER
BEGIN                    ┌ file names essential
  WRITELN (OUTPUT, 'range please');
  READLN (INPUT, j, k);
  ┌FOR i:=j TO k DO ← file name optional
  └ WRITELN ( OUTPUT, i, SQR(i))
  END.
```

Results may be sent to files other than the one named OUTPUT. Each such file must be nominated in the PROGRAM statement and its *type* declared in the VAR section. But OUTPUT should always be nominated, if only to provide a channel for messages ≈ error messages from the Pascal processor in particular:

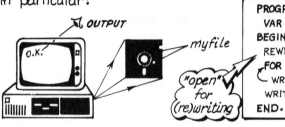

OUTPUT

myfile

"open" for (re)writing

```
PROGRAM  filesquares(OUTPUT, myfile);
  VAR i: INTEGER;  myfile: TEXT
BEGIN                        ┌ file    ┌ file
  REWRITE ( myfile);         │ type    │ name
  ┌FOR i := 1 TO 4 DO
  └ WRITELN (myfile, i, SQR(i));
    WRITELN( OUTPUT, 'O.k.')    ┌ file name
  END.                         │ essential
```

Files other than the file named INPUT may be nominated as sources of data. Each such file must be nominated in the PROGRAM statement and its *type* declaration in the VAR section:

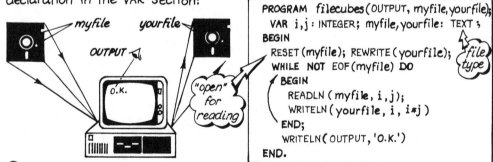

myfile   yourfile

OUTPUT

"open" for reading

```
PROGRAM  filecubes(OUTPUT, myfile, yourfile);
  VAR i,j : INTEGER; myfile, yourfile: TEXT ;
BEGIN
  RESET (myfile); REWRITE ( yourfile);   ┌ file
  WHILE NOT EOF(myfile) DO                │ type
  ┌ BEGIN
  │   READLN ( myfile, i, j);
  │   WRITELN (yourfile, i, i*j )
  └ END;
    WRITELN ( OUTPUT, 'O.K.')
  END.
```

Several files may be open at once; conversely a single file may be opened for writing and subsequently reset for reading all in a single run.

Notice that the files *myfile* and *yourfile* had to be "opened" by REWRITE before writing; by RESET before reading. But REWRITE and RESET may *not* be employed to open the special files named OUTPUT and INPUT which are opened automatically. It is an error to try to open a file already open.

All files in ISO Pascal are *sequential* files. A file opened for writing is initially empty, comprising just an end-of-file mark. Each WRITE or WRITELN causes new information to be appended, then the end-of-file mark to be moved to the new end of file. WRITELN (as distinct from WRITE) causes an end-of-line character to be appended before control moves on.

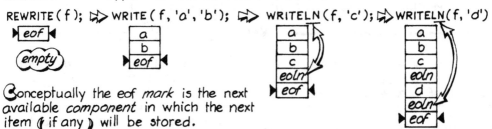

REWRITE(f); ▷ WRITE (f, 'a', 'b'); ▷ WRITELN(f, 'c'); ▷WRITELN(f, 'd')

Conceptually the eof *mark* is the next available *component* in which the next item (if any) will be stored.

A file opened for reading has a "window" placed over its first component. The first READ to be obeyed causes the item in the window to be read, then the window to be moved to the next component, and so on. READLN (as distinct from READ) causes the window to be moved *past the next end-of-line character* before control moves on. If there is no such character the window ends up at the end-of-file mark.

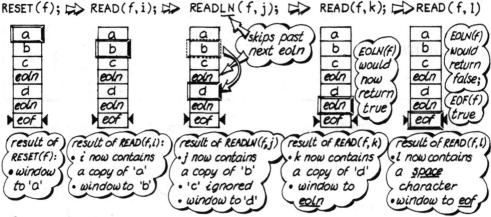

RESET(f); ▷ READ(f, i); ▷ READLN(f, j); ▷ READ(f, k); ▷READ(f, l)

The READ(f, i); READLN(f, j) above could be combined as READLN(f, i, j). In general:

    READLN (f, p, q, r, ...) ≡ READ(f, p); READ(f, q); READ(f, r); ... READLN (f)
    WRITELN (f, p, q, r, ...) ≡ WRITE(f, p); WRITE(f, q); WRITE (f, r); ... WRITELN (f)

The behaviour of the end-of-line character is relevant only to *TEXT* files such as those depicted opposite. A *TEXT* file comprises rows of words and numbers separated by spaces as the name suggests. *Binary* files are explained later.

With *interactive* input the above logic is modified as explained in the next chapter.

113

OPENING FILES

Every file written or read by a Pascal program should be nominated in the PROGRAM statement :

PROGRAM $name_{prog}$ ($name_{file}$) ;

▶ PROGRAM myprog(OUTPUT, mydata, mydump);

always to be nominated

The *type* of each file should be declared in the VAR section of the main program. The syntax is given below, where FILE OF REAL anticipates the subject of *binary files* dealt with later :

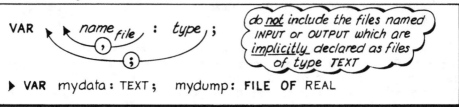

VAR $name_{file}$: $type$;

do __not__ include the files named INPUT or OUTPUT which are __implicitly__ declared as files of type TEXT

▶ VAR mydata : TEXT; mydump: **FILE OF** REAL

A file other than the file named OUTPUT may be written only when it has been opened by invoking the REWRITE procedure :

REWRITE ($name_{file}$)

possibly some local extensions

do not REWRITE the file named OUTPUT

▶ REWRITE (mydump)

A file other than the file named INPUT my be read by READ or READLN only when it has been opened by invoking the RESET procedure.

RESET ($name_{file}$)

possibly some local extensions

do not RESET the file named INPUT

▶ RESET (mydata)

The WRITE, WRITELN, READ, READLN procedures are elaborated on the next double page.

The above definitions apply both to TEXT files and binary files. Binary files are introduced later.

TEXT FILES

The files named INPUT and OUTPUT are of type TEXT. Files nominated by the programmer may also be declared as files of type TEXT.

```
PROGRAM ( INPUT, OUTPUT, hisfile, herfile );
    VAR hisfile, herfile :  TEXT ;
```
TEXT files declared by programmer

A text file consists of ASCII characters ⇌ or characters of whatever code the computer uses ⇌ so a text file is intelligible to the human eye when printed:

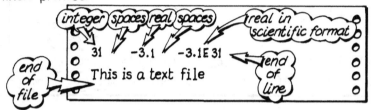

integer *spaces* *real* *spaces* *real in scientific format*

```
31      -3.1     -3.1E 31
This is a text file
```
end of file *end of line*

A text file is organized as rows of items, the items separated by spaces. A Pascal program designed to read such a file may do so one character at a time, using only READ(file, ch) (where *ch* is of type CHAR). Alternatively the program may employ several parameters in its READ statements, each parameter of the same type as that of the corresponding item expected in the text file. For example READLN (file, i, x, y) would correctly read the top line of the text file above (where i is of type INTEGER and x and y of type REAL).

It is the unique property of text files that items are automatically converted from internal form to character form by WRITE, from character form to internal form by READ, as indicated by the *types* of parameters involved. A reading program stops if types fail to match, so it is safer to read data one character at a time and forgo automatic conversion. An input procedure like this is given on pages 118 to 123.

Text files may be created by WRITE statements as illustrated on page 112. Text files may also be typed at the keyboard and stored on disk. The way to do this depends on your installation; consult your local manuals. Typically the file is typed under control of a "line editor" or "screen editor". Such an editor provides facilities for typing, amending, inserting and erasing text. When a file has been typed and corrected it may be saved on disk for subsequent use as the INPUT file for a Pascal program. The command is typically:

```
SAVE  'INPUT'
```
perhaps without the quotes

With many compilers it is not enough to nominate files in the PROGRAM statement; you have also to associate those names with file names recognized by the operating system. *Pro Pascal* and *Turbo Pascal* provide the ASSIGN procedure for this; *Acornsoft ISO Pascal* extends the RESET and REWRITE procedures:

file name for Pascal

```
ASSIGN ( mydata2, 'MYDAT2.TX' )
RESET ( mydata2, 'MYDAT2.TX' )
```
file name for operating system

WRITE AND WRITELN WITH TEXT FILES IN MORE DETAIL

The syntax of the WRITE and WRITELN procedures is:

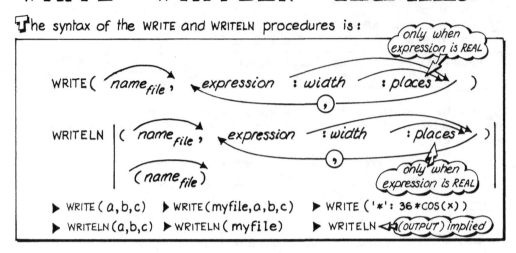

The first WRITE or WRITELN to be obeyed locates the first output field at the start of the output file. ⟨ A *field* is a contiguous sequence of character positions in which an item of output is written ≈ right justified. ⟩ Subsequent fields, and fields generated by subsequent WRITE and WRITELN procedures, are appended sequentially and contiguously as each, in its turn, is written to the output file.

An unspecified *width* for a field of type REAL or INTEGER implies a default width which is installation dependent ⟨ 14 is typical ⟩. An unspecified number of *places* for a field of type REAL implies output in "scientific" form ⟨ E-format ⟩; for example $-1.23456E-04$ to express the value -0.000123456. The number of significant digits printed before the E is installation dependent ⟨ 6 or 9 is typical ⟩. An unspecified *width* for a string implies the number of characters in the string excluding opening and closing apostrophes ⟨ 'abc' implies 3 ⟩. An unspecified *width* for an item of type PACKED ARRAY [1..n] OF CHAR implies n. An unspecified *width* for a Boolean item implies a width which is installation dependent ⟨ typically 4 for TRUE, 5 for FALSE ⟩. A field is extended rightwards if a given value for *width* is too small to accommodate the corresponding item.

When the final parameter of a WRITELN ⟨ as distinct from a WRITE ⟩ procedure has been written, an end-of-line character is automatically appended. WRITELN without a parameter also causes an end-of-line character to be appended.

PAGE WITH TEXT FILES AND ONLY WITH TEXT FILES

The syntax of the PAGE procedure is:

When this standard procedure is invoked a page-throw code is sent to the nominated or implied output file. ⟨ Applicable only if the local equipment can respond to such a signal. ⟩

READ AND READLN WITH TEXT FILES IN MORE DETAIL

The syntax of the READ and READLN procedures is:

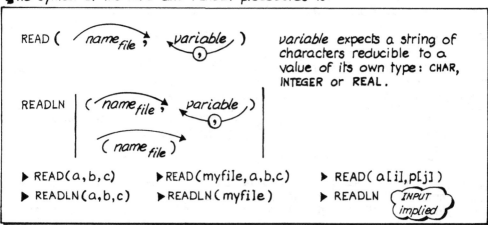

READ ($name_{file}$; $variable$) $variable$ expects a string of characters reducible to a value of its own type: CHAR, INTEGER or REAL.

READLN ($name_{file}$; $variable$)

($name_{file}$)

▶ READ(a,b,c)   ▶ READ(myfile,a,b,c)   ▶ READ(a[i],p[j])
▶ READLN(a,b,c)   ▶ READLN(myfile)   ▶ READLN *INPUT implied*

When the current parameter is of type CHAR the character in the window is read. If this is an end-of-line character it is read as though it were a *space*. It is nevertheless distinguishable from a *space* because whenever there is an end-of-line character in the window ⇄ and at no other time ⇄ the EOLN function for that file would return *true* if invoked. After the character in the window has been read successfully, the window moves on to frame the very next character. If this character happens to be the end-of-file mark then the EOF function for that file would return *true* if invoked. The EOF function returns *true* only when the window is framing the end-of-file mark. Trying to *read* the end-of-file mark is an error.

When the current parameter is of type INTEGER or REAL the window skips over spaces and new lines until the first significant character of a new string is encountered 《 or the search ends abortively at the end-of-file mark 》. A string is converted 《 if correctly formed 》 to an item of standard type consistent with its corresponding parameter. 《 The instruction READ(x), for example, would fail if the string were 1.5 and x of type INTEGER.》 After successful reading of a string the window is made to frame the character immediately following that string. This following character could be a space. Or it could be a new-line character in which case EOLN, if invoked, would return *true* 《 and EOLN *false* 》.

When the final parameter of READLN 《 as distinct from READ 》 has been satisfied the window skips over everything remaining on the current line. It then rests, framing the *first* character of the *next* line. This first character could be the end-of-file mark in which case the EOF function, if invoked, would return *true*. The same applies to READLN when used without parameters.

With text files this conceptual window has an elastic frame. Much of the time it frames only single characters, but when a string of characters denoting a *number* is encountered the frame "s t r e t c h e s" to encompass all characters in that string. This is in contrast to the windows used for reading *binary* files; such windows may be complicated in structure but not elastic. Binary files are described later.

SAFE READING

We have all had to complete a "formated" data form from time to time. It has advantages, if only in making life easier for the programmer:

But when the data are complicated it is sensible to make the arrangement of data more flexible. The programmer

```
Weight ⌐.⌐⌐ kg
Radii X ⌐.⌐⌐  Y ⌐.⌐⌐ cm
Serial Number ⌐⌐⌐⌐⌐
```

may devise a "problem-oriented language" in which a keyword tells the program what the next number, or group of numbers, describes:

```
WEIGHT  16.75
   RADII  X 2  Y 3.62
      SERIAL  54321
```

same data

```
SERI, 54321,  WEIGHT, 16.75
RADIUSES
Y 3.62,  X 2
```

In a program designed to read "formated" data it is conceivable that the programmer would leave verification of data to Pascal; for example by employing READ(INPUT, weight) to read the first item in the top data sheet above. But if the user of such a program erroneously entered 16.7S, say, instead of 16.75 there would be a message from Pascal about a bad number ≈ and the program would stop. For a program that reads more than a few items of data such an approach is unthinkable.

The only way for a program to stay in control is to read data one character at a time, building up the number or keyword and discovering the user's errors for itself. The only pre-defined Pascal procedure safe to employ is READ(file, ch) preceded by a check on end-of-file.

If this conclusion shows Pascal in a bad light be assured that several other established languages are no better in their handling of input. Fortran offers a tempting range of input descriptors (see my *Illustrating Fortran, C.U.P, 1982, ch 10*) but the only usable one is that which reads a single character. Those versions of BASIC that have "ON ERROR..." are a little more helpful because this statement makes it possible to win back control when a bad item has been read; a clumsy approach.

The procedure described below is designed to stay in control whatever nonsense has been encountered on the input file. The procedure is called *grab*.

To use *grab* simply invoke it whenever the next item is needed; there is no need to check the end-of-file before invocation. Each item is deemed to be terminated by a *space, newline* or *end-of-file*. The procedure returns with a record describing every aspect of the item just read. The four kinds of item distinguished by *grab* are:

- *name*; a name begins with a letter and comprises only letters and digits. Only the first four characters are significant (RADII ≡ RADIUSES)

- *number*; a number may be written with or without a decimal point; the procedure distinguishes one form of number from the other

- *nogood*; a string of characters which is neither name or number (for example +P6)

- *tisn't*; a null item implying end-of-file (any subsequent invocation of *grab* would then cause the same result).

The record with which the procedure ⇨ returns is depicted here. It looks complicated but is very simple to use. Suppose, for example, the programmer expects the next item from the input file to be a number. The invocation might be: 🔍

```
grab( it );
IF      it.tisnumber
  THEN    remember := it.nr
  ELSE    complain( it );
```

where we assume that *complain* is a diagnostic procedure. So if the item proved to be something other than a number the diagnostic procedure could discover precisely what went wrong (IF it.tisnt THEN...   IF it.tisnogood THEN...) and might investigate precisely what the user typed by consulting the component *it.string*.

```
·string  [................]⌇ ]72
·length  [      1..72
·nr      [                    ] REAL
·int     [             ] INTEGER
·nom     [     ]
·tisnumber  []
·tisinteger []
·tisname    []   BOOLEAN
·tisnogood  []    "flags"
·tisnt      []
```
(this is the type of record used by grab)

The programmer would probably employ: WITH it DO... and so simplify references to the record thus: IF tisnumber THEN...   IF tisnogood THEN...

A number such as 12345 on the input file causes *both* the flag *tisnumber* and the flag *tisinteger* to be set *true*; a value of 12345.0 would then be found in field *·nr* and a value of 12345 in field *·int*. But 12345000000 on the input file would cause only *tisnumber* to be set *true* because (on a typical computer) this value would be greater than MAXINT.

Here is the essential logic of the *grab* procedure expressed as a state table. Use of such a table is explained on page 50.

symbol state	$\oplus$ 1]	$\ominus$ 2]	'0'..'9' 3]	'A'..'Z' 'a'..'z' 4]	$\odot$. 5]	other 6]	$\bigodot$, space, newline 7]
⇨[1,	⇨[2,	sign:=-1 ⇨[2, ①	nr:= digit(ch) ⇨[3,	nom[1]:=ch ⇨[6, ⑩	⇨[7,	⇨[7,	⇨[1,
[2,	⇨[7,	⇨[7,	action 2	⇨[7,	⇨[7,	⇨[7,	tisnumber:= TRUE nr:=sign*nr ③ — IF nr<MAXINT then
[3,	⇨[7,	⇨[7,	nr:=10*nr+digit(ch) ⇨[3, ④	⇨[7,	frac⑤ := 1 ⇨[4,	⇨[7,	tisinteger:= TRUE and int:= sign*TRUNC(nr)
[4,	⇨[7,	⇨[7,	frac := 10*frac; ⁻nr:=nr+digit(ch)/frac; ⇨[7, ⑥	⇨[7,	⇨[7,	⇨[7,	tisnogood := TRUE ⑦
[5,	⇨[7,	⇨[7,	⇨[5,	⇨[7,	⇨[7,	⇨[7,	tisnumber:= TRUE; nr := sign*nr ⑧
[6,	⇨[7,	⇨[7,	i:=i+1; nom[i]:=ch; ⇨[6, ⑪	⇨[7,	⇨[7,	⇨[7,	tisname:=TRUE ⑨
[7,	⇨[7,	⇨[7,	⇨[7,	⇨[7,	⇨[7,	⇨[7,	tisnogood := TRUE ⑦

In this table the various *actions* are numbered in little clouds thus⑦. Changes of *state* are indicated by broad arrows thus ⇨[7,. The table itself is stored as array table[1..7, 1..7] (overleaf) and the number in each component is encoded as:

$$100 * action + state$$

This table is created in the computer with the help of a file.

119

GRAB (record) PROCEDURE FOR SAFE READING

The main program begins by setting constants. *Stringlength* should be as long as the longest possible line of input (in case the user forgets to type any spaces or commas). *Namelength* should be set to the number of significant characters in a name, four being typical. *Minord* and *maxord* are the ordinal values of the first and last character in the available character set. 32 and 127 are for ASCII code; change these if you are using EBCDIC or other code.

file

```
PROGRAM  saferead ( INPUT, OUTPUT, f );
   CONST
      stringlength= 72;  namelength=4;  minord= 32;  maxord=127;
   TYPE
      stringtype = PACKED ARRAY [ 1.. stringlength] OF CHAR;
      nametype=  PACKED ARRAY [ 1.. namelength ] OF CHAR;
      lookuptype = ARRAY [minord.. maxord ] OF 1..7;
      tabletype = ARRAY [ 1..7 , 1..7 ] OF 1..1200;

      intype = RECORD
                  string :  stringtype;
                  length:  0.. stringlength;
                  nr: REAL;
                  int: INTEGER;
                  nom: nametype;
                  tisnumber, tisinteger, tisname,
                  tisnogood, tisnt : BOOLEAN
               END;

   VAR
      it: intype;  lookup: lookuptype;  table: tabletype;
      i : INTEGER;  f: TEXT;        TEXT file
```

lookup[32] 6
lookup[33] 6
lookup[34] 6

lookup[46] 5   "."

lookup[57] 4   "9"

lookup[66] 4   "B"

(examples)

The arrays named *lookup* and *table* have to be initialized. The purpose of *lookup* is to provide the column number of *table* corresponding to the character just read. For example, if the character stored in *ch* were "9" then *lookup[ORD(ch)]* would return 4 directly. Similarly if *ch* contained "." then *lookup[ORD(ch)]* would return 5. Initialization is performed by a special procedure which should be invoked precisely once before subsequent invocations of *grab*. Here is the procedure:

```
PROCEDURE  initialization ( VAR l:lookuptype; VAR t: tabletype);
   VAR
      c: CHAR;  i,j:  1..7;  k: minord.. maxord;
   BEGIN
      FOR k := minord TO maxord DO l[k]:= 6 ;
         l[ORD('+')] := 1;    l[ ORD('-')] := 2 ;
      FOR c := '0' TO '9' DO l[ ORD(c)] := 3;
      FOR c := 'A' TO 'Z' DO l[ ORD(c)] := 4;
      FOR c := 'a' TO 'z' DO l[ ORD(c)] := 4;
         l[ORD('.')] := 5;
         l[ORD (',')] := 7;
         l[ORD (' ')] := 7;
```

fill with sixes, then overwrite some of them

READ(ch) reads the e.o.l character as a space

120

The VAR declaration in the main program contains " f: TEXT " declaring a file of type TEXT. Writing this file and reading it back again avoids the need for forty-nine individual assignments:

$$t[1,1] := 002; \quad t[1,2] := 102; \quad t[1,3] := 203; \quad etc.$$

(If your Pascal compiler permits "temporary" files it may be possible to remove all references to f from the main program and put them in the VAR section of this initialization procedure ≈ the only place where f is used.)

```
REWRITE (f);          ← open for writing to file f
WRITE ( f, 002, 102, 203, 1006, 007, 007, 001 );
WRITE ( f, 007, 007, 203, 007, 007, 007, 300 );
WRITE ( f, 007, 007, 403, 007, 504, 007, 300 );
WRITE ( f, 007, 007, 605, 007, 007, 007, 700 );
WRITE ( f, 007, 007, 605, 007, 007, 007, 800 );
WRITE ( f, 007, 007, 1106, 1106, 007, 007, 900 );
WRITE ( f, 007, 007, 007, 007, 007, 007, 700 );

RESET (f);          ← reset for reading
FOR i := 1 TO 7 DO
    FOR j := 1 TO 7 DO
        READ ( f, t[i,j] );
END;  { initialization }
```

compare this table with that on page 119

key: 504

action 5 ↗ ↖ new state

⇨[0, implies exit

⇨[4,

The start of the grab procedure is shown below. This includes the definition of a local function for returning the integer value of a character; for example *digit ('6')* would return 6.

```
PROCEDURE  grab( VAR rec: intype );
    VAR
        i : 1..stringlength;  sign : -1..1;   state : 0..7;
        ch : CHAR;    action : 0.. 11;   frac : INTEGER;

    FUNCTION  digit (c : CHAR ): INTEGER;
    BEGIN
        digit :=  ORD ( ch ) - ORD ( '0' )
    END;

    BEGIN   { grab }
        WITH  rec  DO
        BEGIN     { WITH rec }

            tisnumber := FALSE;  tisinteger := FALSE;
            tisname := FALSE;  tisnogood := FALSE;  tisnt := FALSE;
            length := 0;  state := 1;  sign := 1;
        ↻ FOR  i := 1 TO stringlength DO  string[i] := ' ';
        ↻ FOR i := 1 TO namelength DO  nom[i] := ' ';
            i := 1;     ← re-initialize
```

set all flags false

blank out the receiving string

continued overleaf

121

Here is the logic of the *grab* procedure:

```
      REPEAT  { for each digit }
        IF  EOF ( INPUT )
          THEN
            BEGIN
              action := table [ state, 7 ] DIV 100;
              tisnt := ( state = 1 )
            END
          ELSE
            BEGIN
              READ ( INPUT, ch );
              length := length+1;  string [ length ] := ch;
              action := table [ state, lookup [ ORD(ch) ] ] DIV 100;
              state := table [ state, lookup [ ORD(ch) ] ] MOD 100
            END;   { END of IF }
        CASE action OF
          0:            ;
          1: sign := -1 ;
          2: nr := digit ( ch );
          3: BEGIN
                IF nr <=  MAXINT
                  THEN
                    BEGIN
                      tisinteger := TRUE;
                      int := sign * TRUNC ( nr )
                    END;
                tisnumber := TRUE;
                nr := sign * nr
             END;
          4: nr := 10 * nr + digit ( ch );
          5: frac := 1;
          6: BEGIN
                frac := 10 * frac;
                nr := nr + digit(ch) / frac
             END;
          7: tisnogood := TRUE;
          8: BEGIN
                tisnumber := TRUE;
                nr := sign * nr
             END;
          9: tisname := TRUE;
         10: nom [1] := ch;
         11: BEGIN
                i := i + 1;
                IF i <= namelength THEN nom[i] := ch·
             END
        END  { CASE }
      UNTIL ( state = 0 ) OR tisnt
    END
  END;  { procedure grab }
```

7 heads the column of terminators

e.o.f when in state 1 means that grab grabbed nothing ... a null item

check end of file

this is the only READ statement in grab

store the string

action and new state

do nothing

was pre-set to +1

first digit

nr can be converted to an integer by TRUNC( ) only if in range of MAXINT

build integer in nr

after the decimal point divide successive digits by 10, 100, 1000 etc.

first character of nom

usual ending

build nom as far as namelength

the e.o.f was met before any item

The following main program is just for demonstrating the procedure named *grab* :

```
BEGIN    { main program }
   initialization ( lookup, table );
   REPEAT
     grab (it);
     WITH  it  DO
       BEGIN

         IF tisnumber THEN  WRITELN ( nr );
         IF tisinteger THEN  WRITELN (int) ;
         IF tisname THEN WRITELN (nom);

         IF tisnogood  THEN
            FOR i := 1 TO length DO
               WRITE ( string [i] );
         WRITELN
       END { WITH it }
   UNTIL  it.tisnt

END.    { program }
```

Experiment with the program as suggested below:

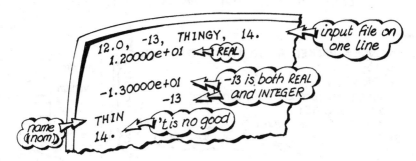

Binary files are introduced on the next page. The file named *f* in the above example would be better as a binary file. To make the alteration change f:TEXT in the main VAR section to f: FILE OF INTEGER .

The check for EOF at the top of the opposite page is there for non-interactive applications but should cause no trouble when *grab* is used interactively. EOF should return *false* unless some special signal (CTRL Z in Turbo Pascal) is sent from the keyboard. If you do have trouble with *grab* consult chapter 11 for inspiration.

INTRODUCING BINARY FILES AND PUT( ) AND GET( )

An item on a *text* file is converted from a character string to internal form by READ; from internal form to a character string by WRITE. By contrast a *binary file* holds data in internal (binary) form. Binary files have several advantages over text files. They are faster to read and write because there is no need for conversion; they are also more compact than text files and suffer none of the rounding errors associated with conversion to and from internal form. A disadvantage of binary files (with the exception of FILE OF CHAR) is that they would be incomprehensible to the human eye if printed.

Binary files are useful as backing storage during computations. Usually such files may be deleted at the end of a run, having served their purpose. But in some applications huge files of intermediate data have to be saved between runs. Binary files, being compact and accurate, are ideal for this purpose.

In Pascal a file is a *variable*. Notice the last line of the VAR section on page 120, reproduced below:

```
     i : INTEGER;   f : TEXT;
```
variable of type TEXT

which shows *f* declared as a variable of type TEXT in precisely the same way as *i* is declared a variable of type INTEGER. In general, files may be of any type ; those *not* of type TEXT being *binary* files.

Here is a file named *binfile*. Each component is a record of the shape used in the program of personnel records on page 102.

```
TYPE
   nametype = PACKED ARRAY [1..10] OF CHAR;
   detailtype =
     RECORD
       surname, forename : nametype;
       age : 18..65;
       grade : ( jr, sr, exec )
     END;
VAR
   binfile : FILE OF detailtype;
```

one component

.surname ⬚
.forename ⬚
. age ⬚
.grade ⬚

Note: "FILE OF"

A single empty component of *binfile* is sketched above. The file comprises many such records as needed during the course of a run.

Declaration of any file has the additional effect of declaring a *window variable* associated with that file. The name of the window is the name of the file, but with ↑ appended as illustrated here: ⬚
All communication with the file named *binfile* is through the window named *binfile↑* which you pronounce as " binfile-window ".

binfile↑. surname ⬚
binfile↑.forename ⬚
binfile↑.age ⬚
binfile↑.grade ⬚

The syntax for type of file is defined as follows:

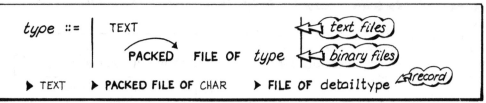

Do not confuse FILE OF CHAR with TEXT. Automatic conversions to and from character strings ≈ and detection of end-of-line ≈ are properties exclusively of TEXT files. WRITELN and READLN work only with TEXT files.

Writing a binary file is, in general, a two-stage process: (i) assign to the window-variable whatever is to be written (ii) invoke PUT to move the window frame onwards and establish a new end-of-file:

```
REWRITE ( binfile );
WITH  binfile↑  DO
   BEGIN
      surname := 'VENTANA';
      forename := 'ABIERTA';
      age := 21;
      grade := sr
   END;
PUT ( binfile );
```

empty file; window shows e.o.f

PUT window over new e.o.f.

PUT (name_file)

Having checked for end-of-file, reading is also a two-stage process: (i) read what is in the window (ii) use GET to move the window frame onwards to the next component (⟨ or to the end-of-file if there is no next component ⟩) :

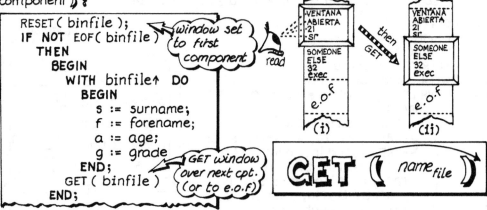

```
RESET ( binfile );
IF NOT EOF ( binfile )
   THEN
      BEGIN
         WITH binfile↑ DO
            BEGIN
               s := surname;
               f := forename;
               a := age;
               g := grade
            END;
         GET ( binfile )
      END;
```

window set to first component

GET window over next cpt. (or to e.o.f.)

GET (name_file)

Procedures PUT and GET are "low level" procedures. WRITE and READ may be described in terms of PUT and GET ≈ and the window variable ≈ as follows:

```
WRITE ( filename, item ) ≡  filename↑ := item ;  PUT ( filename )
READ  ( filename, item ) ≡  item := filename↑;  GET ( filename )
```

Turbo Pascal does not define PUT or GET; it has extended WRITE & READ instead.

125

COMPRESSION

This program is designed to read a text file and write a corresponding binary file, so compressing the information held.

Assume the text file has already been verified by another program so that no checks on form or completeness need be made on input; the file is known to be strictly of the form illustrated ⇒

SUN-ROOM temperature log

Day No.	Month	Noon temp	Remarks
2	FEB	2·5	COLD
4	FEB	–10	BITTER
17	FEB	–15·5	8 MONKEYS

```
PROGRAM compressor( textin, binaryout, OUTPUT );
   CONST
      monthchars = 3;
      remchars = 8;

   TYPE
      monthtype = PACKED ARRAY [1..monthchars] OF CHAR;
      remtype = PACKED ARRAY [1..remchars] OF CHAR;
      grouptype = RECORD
                     day: 1..31;
                     month: monthtype;
                     temp: REAL;
                     remark: remtype
                  END;

   VAR
      textin: TEXT;
      binaryout: FILE OF grouptype;
      count: INTEGER;  i: 1..monthchars;  j: 1..remchars;

   BEGIN
      count := 0;
      RESET( textin );
      REWRITE( binaryout );
      WITH binaryout↑ DO
         WHILE NOT EOF( textin ) DO
            BEGIN
               READ( textin, day);
               FOR i := 1 TO monthchars DO
                  READ( textin, month[i]);
               READ( textin, temp );
               FOR j := 1 TO remchars DO
                  READ( textin, remark[j]);
               count := count + 1;
               READLN( textin );
               PUT( binaryout)
            END { WHILE }
      { end of WITH }
      WRITELN( OUTPUT, count, ' lines of data transferred' )

   END.
```

messages

•day [ ] 1..31
•month
•temp • REAL
•remark

grouptype

binaryout

window

binaryout↑ . day
binaryout↑ . month
binaryout↑ . temp
binaryout↑ . remark

PUT

SUMMARY OF PROPERTIES OF FILES

PROPERTY \ TYPE OF FILE	TEXT FILES — The standard TEXT files: INPUT and OUTPUT	TEXT FILES — Names given by the programmer	PACKED FILE OF CHAR (not TEXT files)	Other types (e.g. files of ARRAYS; files of RECORDS of mixed type)
Inclusion of file names in the PROGRAM statement	INPUT is optional but OUTPUT must be included if only to give a destination for error reports	In general the file should be nominated in the PROGRAM statement. (Some compilers permit "temporary" files, these not being nominated in the PROGRAM statement)		
Definition of file variable in VAR section	Implicitly of type TEXT	In general the file variable should be declared in the main VAR section (a local VAR section if the compiler allows "temporary" files)		
RESET and REWRITE	Implicit: do not use RESET or REWRITE	Files to be read must be opened using RESET (filename). Files to be written must first be opened using REWRITE (filename)		
Input statements available	READ, READLN and GET: Omitting first parameter implies INPUT	READ, READLN and GET: No default parameter	READ and GET but not READLN	
Conversions on input	Each character-string encoded automatically as CHAR, INTEGER, or REAL to match the basic type of the receiving parameter		Binary code on file converted to items of type CHAR only	Binary code on file converted to INTEGER, REAL or CHAR according to type of file variable
Output statements available	WRITE, WRITELN, PUT and PAGE (but some Pascal compilers do not offer PUT)		WRITE and PUT but not WRITELN	
Conversions on output	Items of type CHAR, INTEGER, BOOLEAN — also PACKED ARRAY OF CHAR — are converted to printable character strings		Items of type CHAR converted to binary code on output file	Items of all types converted to binary code on output file
EOLN	The end-of-line character is read as a space but causes EOLN( ) to return TRUE whilst the end-of-line character is in the file window		End of line is not detectable; the EOLN( ) function is relevant only to TEXT files	
	EOLN implies EOLN (INPUT)	No default parameter		
EOF	The EOF function returns TRUE if invoked whilst the end-of-file "mark" is in the file window, otherwise it returns FALSE			
	EOF implies EOF (INPUT)	No default parameter for EOF( )		
	With interactive input the EOF signal is installation dependent		Interactive input is infeasible	

EXERCISES

1. Implement the *saferead* program. Experiment by trying to "break" it from the keyboard. It should be found impossible to make the program lose control; on each attempt the erroneous string would be displayed for inspection

2. Make the *personnel* program on page 102 file the array of personnel records (array a) as a binary file. The file should be written when all the data have been read and before they have been sorted. Similarly make the program start by reading such a file before the input of each new batch of records. With these facilities the program begins to look like a rudimentary management system.

3. Take any of the programs in earlier chapters (for example the *loanrate* program on page 62) and replace its primitive input statements with invocations of the *grab* procedure. If your Pascal permits interactive programs add suitable prompts and error diagnostics to make the resulting program reasonably friendly towards its intended user.

11

INTERACTIVE INPUT

INTERACTION

A user of many modern programs takes part in a dialogue, the program displaying questions or prompts on the screen, the user responding by typing at the keyboard. Each response is made in the light of results so far displayed on the screen. There might be a different result if the user had to supply all information in advance. In other words the user and the program "interact" to achieve a result. The concept of interaction is commonplace now but its achievement is comparatively recent in the history of computing.

Pascal was designed before interaction became commonplace. It was designed in the days when programmers punched programs into cards, surrendering a "program deck" to computer operators for loading into the card reader. The data were also punched into cards and handed to the operators as a "data deck". Both decks were later returned to the programmer wrapped in "music paper" with results (or woeful diagnostics) from the line printer. Because it was usual for the operators to wait until they had acquired several such programs before loading them, this mode of operation was called "batch mode".

The READ procedure of Pascal was designed for the convenience of programmers working in batch mode. The logic of the READ procedure in the context of punched cards is: (i) read the specified item or items from the current card, then (ii) peep ahead to see if there is a further character position on the current card; make EOLN *true* if not. This logic enables the programmer to precede each READ with:

    IF NOT EOLN THEN ...

The logic for reading a whole line (READLN) is similar: (i) read the specified item or items from the current card, ignoring any remaining character positions, then (ii) peep ahead to see if there is a further card; make EOF *true* if not. This logic enabled the programmer to precede each READLN with:

    IF NOT EOF THEN ...

But when input is interactive, peeping ahead is nonsense; a program can't know what its user intends to type next. So the logic of READ and READLN has to be modified wherever the source of input is to be a human being responding to prompts.

A popular modification (Acornsoft: ISO Pascal, Prospero: Pro Pascal) is "lazy i/o" which means delaying the peep ahead until the program makes a further reference ≈ e.g. by READ or EOF ≈ to the keyboard. Another technique (Borland: Turbo Pascal) is to treat the *current* character from a keyboard as the result of the peep ahead. Both methods solve the peep ahead problem demonstrated opposite. Other problems follow.

PEEP-AHEAD PROBLEM

*I*nteractive hiccups are caused by the logic of peeping ahead as discussed in general opposite. The RESET procedure (implicit in the case of INPUT) places a window over the first item of the file; the subsequent READ or READLN procedure copies what is in the window *then moves the window to the next character or past the next end-of-line* respectively. This logic is so fundamental to Pascal that it is worth exploring what would happen if an attempt were made to run this little program — if compiled by a traditional Pascal compiler — interactively.

```pascal
PROGRAM hiccups(INPUT, OUTPUT);
  VAR a, b: CHAR;
BEGIN
  WRITELN ('first please');
  READLN (a);
  WRITELN ('second please');
  READLN (b);
  WRITELN (a, b, '!')
END.
```

*C*ontrol begins at WRITELN('first please') and goes straight on to READLN(a), making the program wait for something to be typed and entered.

*T*ype U and press the RETURN key.

READLN(a) picks up the U but is not satisfied until it has peeped ahead at the first character of the next line. So we are hung up. The obvious thing to do is offer the first character of the next line.

*S*till hanging! In most systems the program receives no data until the RETURN key is pressed. Press it.

*T*hat satisfied READLN(a) so control went on to WRITELN('second please') and so to READLN(b). READLN(b) picked up the P but won't be satisfied until it has peeped ahead to the first character of the next line. Hung up again!

*T*here is no next line. Nevertheless enter something. Anything!

*T*hat satisfied READLN(b) so control went on to WRITELN(a,b,'!') and so to the end of the program. Messy result.

*P*ascal compilers such as those quoted opposite do not cause hiccups; the result would be as one would expect from reading the text of the program. In other words as illustrated here.

BUFFER PROBLEM
IF YOUR PASCAL HAS THIS TROUBLE DON'T WRITE INTERACTIVE PROGRAMS

In the days when the word "file" implied "magnetic-tape file" it was customary for the Pascal processor to employ *buffers* for input and output. A buffer is an area of memory. Characters to be sent to the output file would be sent as far as the buffer; only when the buffer was full would its contents be copied to the magnetic tape. The same idea was employed for input. Such buffering is essential when filing on magnetic tapes, useful when filing on disks, but if the "file" is a person typing at a keyboard buffering is disastrous. The following analysis illustrates such a disaster.

```
PROGRAM flush( INPUT, OUTPUT );
  VAR a, b : CHAR;
BEGIN
  WRITELN( 'first please');
  READ(a);
  WRITELN ('second please');
  READ (b);
  WRITELN ( a, b, '!')
END.
```

Control starts at WRITELN('first please'). The words 'first please' are faithfully written, but written to the output buffer ⇌ which has plenty of room so its contents are not yet copied to the screen. The screen reveals nothing. But the program is waiting.

Type a line of data and press the RETURN key. The data are "echoed" to the screen, but this does not mean the program has received them.

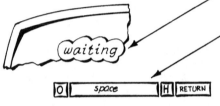

If nothing else happens it means the data have gone to the input buffer and won't come out until the buffer is full or until you send an *e.o.f.* from the keyboard. (The *e.o.f.* signal is installation dependent.)

Assume there is just a *line buffer* for input and that the RETURN key activates it. That means READ(a) is satisfied; WRITELN('second please') sends the words 'second please' to the output buffer; READ(b) is satisfied; WRITELN(a,b,'!') sends the word 'OH!' to the output buffer.

Finally control reaches END. at which stage the output buffer is copied to the screen.

If your programs behave like this it means your Pascal compiler was not designed to compile interactive programs. Programs to be compiled by such a compiler should be designed to read data from a disk file.

Pro Pascal, Turbo Pascal and Acornsoft ISO Pascal do not exhibit the difficulties described above; interactive programs may be compiled by them.

EOF PROBLEM

This is the standard Pascal model for non-interactive input. But what does *EOF* mean in an interactive program? Typically end-of-file is signalled from the keyboard by a special character   particular to each installation. An example end-of-file signal is pressing CTRL and Z together.

```
WHILE NOT EOF(f) THEN
  BEGIN

    • read & process what is in the
      window, then
    • move the window to next item

  END
```

```
PROGRAM pardon ( INPUT, OUTPUT );
  VAR  i : INTEGER ;
BEGIN
  WHILE NOT  EOF(INPUT) DO
    BEGIN
      WRITELN ( 'next please' );
      READLN ( INPUT, i );
      WRITELN ( 'times 2 =', 2*i )
    END
END.
```

Here is what happens if you write an interactive program using this model.

Control begins at WHILE NOT EOF(INPUT) where it hangs. Nothing has yet been typed so there is nothing for EOF to test. (The READLN statement is not to blame because control has not reached a READLN statement yet.) Help the program by entering the first number.

The '11' satisfied the EOF test. EOF(INPUT) returned *false* so control went to WRITELN('next please') and so to the READLN(INPUT, i). The READLN(INPUT,i) picked up the '11' but won't be satisfied until it has peeped ahead (more about this at the bottom of the page).

That satisfied READLN(INPUT, i) for the first number   11   so control went to WRITELN ('times 2 =', 2*i) which wrote 22, then back round the loop to WRITELN('next please'), and so to READLN(INPUT,i). The READLN (INPUT, i) picks up the '12' and waits for the next chance to peep ahead.

Thus the program would continue to print the solution to the problem-before-last, then ask for the number it has just been given.

Until you press the combination of keys that signals end-of-file on your particular installation (shown here as ▓).

With "lazy input" the results look a little less silly but remain out of phase ⇨

Don't use WHILE NOT EOF in interactive programs.

12

DYNAMIC STORAGE

DYNAMIC STORAGE

The concept of a *pointer* has already been introduced in the context of sorting an array. The pointers are exchanged rather than the components they point to. In this context the pointers are *integers* confined to the subrange of the array subscripts.

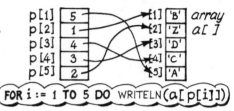

FOR i := 1 TO 5 DO WRITELN(a[p[i]])

Wherever the things to be sorted may be held in a simple array the pointers to those things may be *integers* as demonstrated above. But the use of arrays is not always convenient because the array structure is too rigid. Moss Bros does not stock a morning suit and a dinner jacket for hire to *every* customer on its books because it is unusual for them all to wed on the same day or dine extravagantly on the same evening. By analogy it is not practicable to declare an array of maximum possible size for every array variable. On the hypothesis of the more sheep the less goats Pascal provides a "heap" of storage boxes. As data arrive, boxes may be taken from the heap and assembled into records. If the first item of data is a temperature reading, for example, a container of type REAL is assembled for storing the value. If the next item comprises a complicated personnel record then boxes from the heap are assembled into a container of corresponding TYPE. When a record is no longer wanted its container may be disposed of by throwing its component storage boxes back on the heap. Such records, because they come and go, are called *dynamic records*.

Dynamic records are now introduced by analogy with a *file*. Recall that every file is associated with a *file variable* in the form of a *window*. If the file is named *f* then the window is referred to as *f↑*. In other words a window has no name of its own; it is referred to by the name of the file which comprises a "chain" of such windows ➩

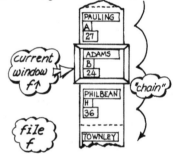

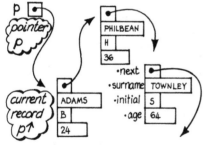

Similarly a *pointer* is associated with every *dynamic record*. If the pointer is named *p* the dynamic record is referred to as *p↑*. In other words a dynamic record has no name of its own; it may be referred to by the name of any pointer which points directly to it. A "chain" may be constructed by giving each record a component for containing the pointer to another.

Items in the current *record* are referred to in the same way as those in the current *window* :

WRITELN(f↑.initial); ≡ WRITELN(p↑.initial); ➩ B

The pointers illustrated here are *not* of type INTEGER, they are items of a special *pointer type* (you can't WRITE a pointer to see what it looks like). The syntax for declaring pointers of pointer type is now defined:

optional spaces   ↑ name type   **POINTER TYPE**   ▶ TYPE   (POINTER TO) pointertype = ↑ persontype

Compare the above syntax of *pointer* type with that of *file* type:

PACKED   FILE OF *type*   **FILE TYPE**   ▶ TYPE   filetype = (FILE OF) persontype

Notice that the words FILE OF are matched *not* by the words POINTER TO (as one might expect) but by an upward arrow. In this context the upward arrow should be pronounced "pointer to" and thought of as shorthand for POINTER TO .

Comparing syntax, the words FILE OF may be followed by the *name* of a type or by *the full definition* of a type. In this example the name *persontype* could be eliminated by placing the RECORD definition directly after FILE OF. But this short cut is *not* allowed with pointers; the item after the upward arrow must be the *name* of a type previously defined.

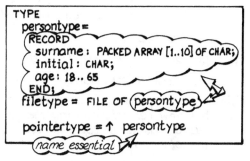

TYPE
persontype =
RECORD
   surname : PACKED ARRAY [1..10] OF CHAR;
   initial : CHAR;
   age: 18..65
END;
filetype = FILE OF (persontype)

pointertype = ↑ persontype
(name essential)

A pointer to a record is of most use if the record itself contains a pointer pointing to another record. The simplest data structure linked by such pointers is the "chain" illustrated opposite. It needs the following pair of declarations:

persontype = RECORD
     next : pointertype;
     surname: PACKED ARRAY [1..10] OF CHAR;
     initial : CHAR;
     age : 18..65
     END;

(POINTER TO)
pointertype = ↑ persontype;

Which should come first? If we declared *persontype* first it would refer forward to *pointertype*; conversely *pointertype* declared first would refer forward to *persontype*. But no Catch 22; declare first the one with the upward arrow. A forward reference from a POINTER TO is permitted as a necessary exception to the rule forbidding references to things yet to be defined.

Having named one or more pointer *types*, pointer *variables* may be declared in the VAR section in the usual way. The example on the next double page shows the declaration of pointer variables named *head* and *p*; both are of the pointer type named *pointertype*.

A standard pointer *constant* is provided, needing no declaration (there is no way to declare pointer constants of one's own). The standard pointer constant is named NIL and is defined below. It is analogous to zero when manipulating pointers and is useful for marking the end of a chain as illustrated on the next double page.

NIL ◄ standard constant of pointer type

NEW AND DISPOSE

To explain what the program on the opposite page does it is easiest to start the explanation part way through. The user entered an 'A', then a 'B' and the program did this:

The user now plans to enter a 'c' for linking to the chain illustrated. The four steps for linking ⟨ already employed to link A and B⟩ are:

(i) create a new record pointed to by p. This is achieved by invoking a standard procedure named NEW:

   NEW(p);

(ii) put data in the record; e.g.

   READLN(p↑. data);

(iii) copy the pointer from *top* into the new record, causing the new record ⟨ as well as *top* ⟩ to head the *old* chain:

   p↑ . next := top;

(iv) copy the pointer from *p* into *top* causing *top* ⟨ as well as *p* ⟩ to head the *augmented* chain:

   top := p;

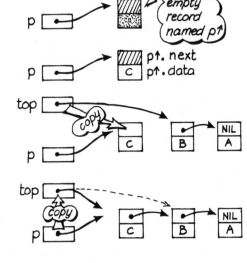

The result is:

To *unlink* the record currently at the head of the chain requires only one step if a bit of memory may be wasted ⟨ as often it may ⟩ :

(i) copy the pointer of the doomed record into *top*, causing *top* to point to the subsequent record:

   top := top↑. next;

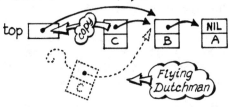

But if Flying Dutchmen cannot be afforded, their hulks may be returned to the heap for re-use. To do this (i) point to the doomed record, (ii) unlink as above, (iii) invoke the standard procedure named DISPOSE. Three steps instead of one:

   p := top;
   top := top↑. next;
   DISPOSE(p)

The 'c' has now vanished; *p* is undefined.

From the explanation opposite it is evident that the last record to be linked is the first to be unlinked. So we can change the metaphor from linking and unlinking a chain to "pushing and popping a stack".

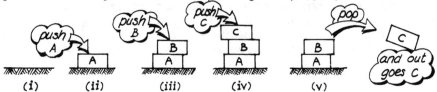

(i)   (ii)   (iii)   (iv)   (v)

To operate the program below: Enter +L (or plus any letter) to push that letter onto the stack; enter a lone minus sign (at the start of a line) to pop the stack. Enter a lone asterisk (at the start of a line) to stop.

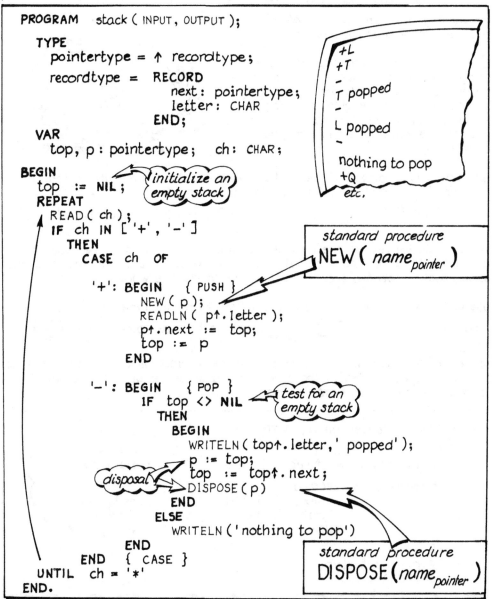

```
PROGRAM    stack ( INPUT, OUTPUT );

   TYPE
      pointertype = ↑ recordtype;

      recordtype =  RECORD
                       next: pointertype;
                       letter: CHAR
                    END;
   VAR
      top, p : pointertype;   ch: CHAR;
BEGIN
   top  := NIL ;          initialize an
                          empty stack
   REPEAT
      READ ( ch );
      IF ch IN [ '+' , '-' ]
         THEN
            CASE ch OF

               '+': BEGIN    { PUSH }
                       NEW ( p );
                       READLN ( p↑.letter );
                       p↑.next :=  top;
                       top :=  p
                    END

               '-': BEGIN    { POP }
                       IF  top <> NIL          test for an
                          THEN                 empty stack
                             BEGIN
                                WRITELN ( top↑.letter,' popped' );
                                p := top;
                                top := top↑.next ;
                                DISPOSE ( p )
                             END
                          ELSE
                             WRITELN ('nothing to pop')
                    END
            END   { CASE }
      UNTIL  ch = '*'
END.
```

Notes on diagram (handwritten panel):

```
+L
+T
-
T popped
-
L popped
-
nothing to pop
+Q
etc.
```

standard procedure
NEW (name$_{pointer}$)

disposal

standard procedure
DISPOSE (name$_{pointer}$)

The program on the previous page was kept as simple as possible to show without distraction the mechanism of linking and unlinking a record to the head of a chain. The program below employs the same techniques but parcelled as functions and procedures to be invoked as follows:

$$push (ptr, ch) \qquad and \qquad ch := pop (ptr)$$

Without altering the simple chain structure of the stack, two further utilities are added:

$$pushtail (ptr, ch) \qquad and \qquad ch := poptail (ptr)$$

for pushing an item on the *bottom* of a stack and popping an item from the *bottom* of a stack respectively.

Using only *push* and *poptail* means using a chain as a *queue*. Items are pushed on at one end, wait in the queue, get popped from the other end for service. Using only *pushtail* and *pop* implies a similar queue in the opposite direction.

Recursion is employed to reach the bottom of the stack. When *pushtail* is invoked the current link of the chain appears in one of two states:

$$ptr \boxed{NIL} \qquad or\ else \qquad ptr \boxed{\bullet} \longrightarrow \boxed{} ptr\uparrow.next$$

If ptr = NIL we are at the end of a chain, so the NIL has to be replaced by a pointer to a new record. If ptr <> NIL we are *not* at the end of a chain so we invoke *pushtail (ptr↑.next , ch)* to do the work.

Recursion is also used in *poptail*, but here there are *three* possible states:

$$ptr \boxed{NIL} \quad or \quad ptr \boxed{\bullet} \longrightarrow \boxed{NIL} ptr\uparrow.next \quad or \quad ptr \boxed{\bullet} \longrightarrow \boxed{\bullet} \longrightarrow$$

If ptr=NIL the queue is empty. If ptr↑.next = NIL there is a solitary item which may be popped as though the queue were a stack. If ptr↑.next <> NIL we invoke *poptail (ptr↑.next)* to do the work.

```
PROGRAM    staque ( INPUT, OUTPUT );
  TYPE
    pointertype  =  ↑recordtype;

    recordtype = RECORD
                   next : pointertype;
                   data : CHAR
                 END;

  VAR
    top: pointertype;
    ch: CHAR;
```

first set up the data structure

•next
•data

```pascal
PROCEDURE push(VAR ptr: pointertype; c: CHAR);
   VAR
      p: pointertype;
   BEGIN
      NEW(p);
      p↑.data := c;
      p↑.next := ptr;
      ptr := p
   END;
```

Here are the four utilities; they are used to good effect in the program on page 144.

```pascal
FUNCTION pop(VAR ptr: pointertype): CHAR;
   BEGIN
      pop := CHR(∅);
      IF ptr <> NIL
         THEN
            BEGIN
               pop := ptr↑.data;
               ptr := ptr↑.next
            END
   END;
```

'pop' returns this invisible character if stack is empty

dispose of the Flying Dutchman if you wish

```pascal
PROCEDURE pushtail(VAR ptr: pointertype; c: CHAR);
   BEGIN
      IF ptr = NIL
         THEN
            BEGIN
               NEW(ptr);
               ptr↑.data := c;
               ptr↑.next := NIL
            END
         ELSE
            pushtail(ptr↑.next, c)
   END;
```

recursion

```pascal
FUNCTION poptail(VAR ptr: pointertype): CHAR;
   BEGIN
      poptail := CHR(∅);
      IF ptr <> NIL
         THEN
            IF ptr↑.next = NIL
               THEN
                  poptail := pop(ptr)
               ELSE
                  poptail := poptail(ptr↑.next)
   END;
```

empty: see above

recursion

```pascal
BEGIN   { staque }
   top := NIL;
   REPEAT
      READ(ch);
      IF ch IN ['+', '-', '>', '<']
         THEN
            CASE ch OF
            '+': BEGIN
                    READLN(ch);
                    push(top, ch)
                 END;

            '-': WRITELN(pop(top));

            '>': BEGIN
                    READLN(ch);
                    pushtail(top, ch)
                 END;

            '<': WRITELN(poptail(top))
            END
   UNTIL ch = '*'
END.
```

push pop pushtail poptail

use this program in the same way as that on page 139 ≈ but enjoy two extra facilities:

+L to push 'L' (for any letter) on the stack

>L to push letter on the bottom of the stack

− to pop the stack

< to pop the bottom of the stack

* to stop

REVERSE POLISH NOTATION

Algebraic expressions in conventional form may be expressed in Reverse Polish Notation which has no parentheses ("Polish" because the notation was devised by the Polish logician Jan Lukaciewicz which only Poles can pronounce; "Reverse" because his original order of operators and operands has been reversed). As an example of reverse Polish notation:

$$A + (B - C) * D - F/(G+H) \quad \text{transforms to} \quad ABC-D*+FGH+/-$$

The reverse Polish expression is easier to evaluate than might appear. For example let A = 6, B = 4, C = 1, D = 2, F = 3, G = 7, H = 5. With these values the expression to be evaluated is :

$$6 \quad 4 \quad 1 \quad - \quad 2 \quad * \quad + \quad 3 \quad 7 \quad 5 \quad + \quad / \quad -$$

Work from left to right taking each item in turn. Whenever you come to an operator *apply it to the previous two terms*, reducing two terms to one:

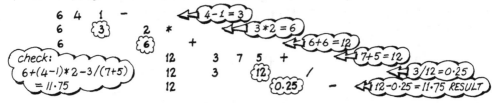

```
6   4   1   -              4-1 = 3
6      {3}      2   *              3*2 = 6
6      {6}          +                  6+6 = 12
check:                 12    3   7   5   +                 7+5 = 12
6+(4-1)*2-3/(7+5)      12    3       {12}      /             3/12 = 0.25
   = 11.75             12                {0.25}   -      12-0.25 = 11.75 RESULT
```

The above should demonstrate that reverse Polish notation would be useful for evaluating expressions by computer. So how do you transform an expression such as A+(B-C)*D-F/(G+H) in the first place? The process employs two stacks; the steps are explained below.

$$A + (B - C) * D - F / (G + H) =$$

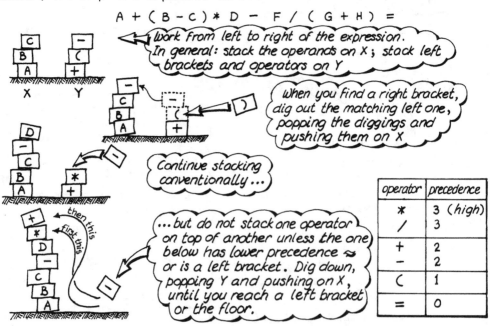

Work from left to right of the expression. In general: stack the operands on X; stack left brackets and operators on Y

When you find a right bracket, dig out the matching left one, popping the diggings and pushing them on X

Continue stacking conventionally ...

... but do not stack one operator on top of another unless the one below has lower precedence ⪯ or is a left bracket. Dig down, popping Y and pushing on X, until you reach a left bracket or the floor.

operator	precedence
*	3 (high)
/	3
+	2
-	2
(	1
=	0

Notice that the left bracket is included in the precedence table and allocated low precedence. This is a trick to avoid having to treat explicitly the condition "⪯ *or is a left bracket*". Clever.

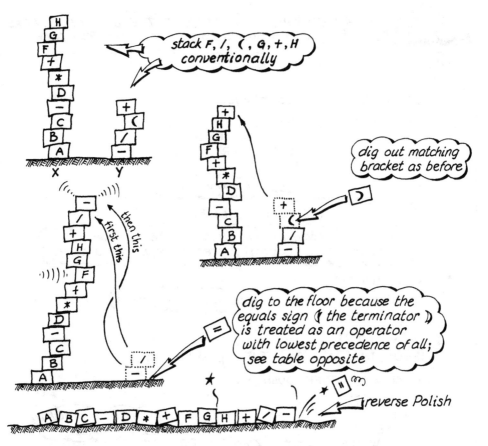

In addition to the procedure *push (stack, ch)* and the functions *pop(stack)* and *poptail(stack)* a function is needed to return the precedence of an operator. The function shown below is given a character as its parameter and returns the corresponding integer from the little table opposite:

```
FUNCTION  prec( c : CHAR ): INTEGER;
  BEGIN
    CASE  c  OF

    '*', '/' :   prec := 3;
    '+', '-' :   prec := 2;
    '(': prec :=  1 ;
    '=': prec :=  0

    END
  END;
```

see little table opposite

On the next page is a program to transform conventional expressions to reverse Polish. To use the program type the expression and terminate with an equals sign:

A+(B-C)*D-F/(G+H)=   enter this

ABC-D*+FGH+/-   get result

143

```
PROGRAM  hsilop ( INPUT, OUTPUT );
   TYPE

      pointertype = ↑ recordtype;

      recordtype = RECORD
                      next:  pointertype;
                      data:  CHAR
                   END;
   VAR                           ← x and y stacks
      x, y : pointertype;
      ch: CHAR;    i : 0..40;   exit: BOOLEAN;

         insert procedures and functions here: use
         push, pop, poptail, prec from previous pages

BEGIN   { hsilop }

   x := NIL;   y := NIL;       ← initialize stacks

   REPEAT
      READ ( ch );

      IF ch  IN [ 'A'..'z' ] THEN  push( x, ch );

      IF ch = '(' THEN  push ( y, ch );

      IF  ch = ')'
         THEN                            ← dig out the matching
            BEGIN                          left bracket
               WHILE y↑. data <> '('  DO
                  push ( x, pop ( y ) );
               ch := pop ( y )            ← then throw it away
            END;

      IF  ch  IN [ '+','−', '*', '/', '=' ]
         THEN
            BEGIN
               REPEAT
                  exit := TRUE;          ← if the precedence of the
                  IF  y <> NIL              operator on top...
                     THEN
                        IF prec( ch ) <= prec( y↑. data )   ... <= precedence
                           THEN                             of the operator
                              BEGIN                         or left bracket
                                 push ( x, pop ( y ));      beneath
                                 exit := FALSE
                              END;
               UNTIL  exit;           ← only then is it
               push ( y, ch )           right to push
            END                         the new operator

   UNTIL ch = '=' ;
                                        ← write out stack
   WHILE x <> NIL DO  WRITE ( poptail ( x ));   from bottom to
   WRITELN                                      top
END.
```

SIMPLE CHAINS

The essence of a *stack* or *queue* is that referring to a record means *removing* that record. (There is cheating in the previous example where the program peeps at the record on top of the stack before deciding to pop it.) But there are many applications in which sequential records of a chain are referred to without removing them. Referring to sequential records in this way is called *traversal*.

Below are shown a conventional chain and a fragment of program for its traversal. "Referring to a record" in this example involves no more than printing an item from one of its components but would, in general, be a more complicated procedure.

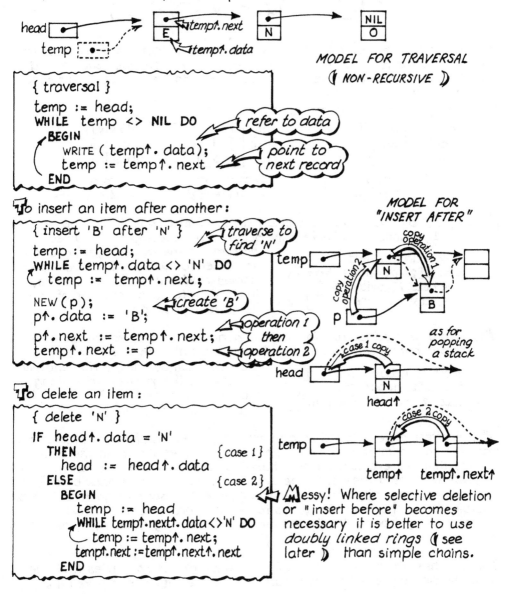

head

temp

MODEL FOR TRAVERSAL
(NON-RECURSIVE)

```
{ traversal }
temp := head;
WHILE  temp <> NIL DO          refer to data
  BEGIN
    WRITE ( temp↑. data);      point to
    temp := temp↑. next        next record
  END
```

To insert an item after another:

MODEL FOR "INSERT AFTER"

```
{ insert 'B' after 'N' }        traverse to
                                find 'N'
temp := head;
WHILE temp↑. data <> 'N'  DO
   temp := temp↑. next;

NEW (p);                        create 'B'
p↑. data := 'B';
p↑. next := temp↑. next;        operation 1
                                then
temp↑. next := p                operation 2
```

as for
popping
a stack

To delete an item:

```
{ delete 'N' }
IF  head↑. data = 'N'
   THEN                      {case 1}
      head := head↑. data
   ELSE                      {case 2}
      BEGIN
        temp := head
        WHILE temp↑.next↑.data<>'N' DO
           temp := temp↑. next;
        temp↑.next :=temp↑.next↑.next
      END
```

Messy! Where selective deletion or "insert before" becomes necessary it is better to use *doubly linked rings* (see later) than simple chains.

145

SHORTEST ROUTE

Finding the shortest (or longest) route through a network is a problem that crops up in various disciplines — one of which is *critical path scheduling* for the control and monitoring of construction projects. Given a network such as that below, the problem is to find the shortest route from the node marked *START* to that marked *END*. The journey must follow the direction of the arrow. The number against each arrow shows the journey time.

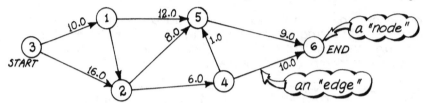

The data structure needed for a shortest-route program is depicted below. There is a record for each *node* and a chain runs from each such record. Each chain comprises *edge* records which store data describing all the edges which run *out* of that node.

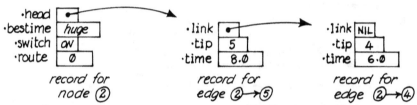

Records for all nodes are held in an array named *nodefacts*. The record for node 2 is annotated more fully below. In the component named

nodefacts[2].head
nodefacts[2].bestime   huge
nodefacts[2].switch   ON
nodefacts[2].route   0

bestime is the value *huge* (a constant set to 10^{20}). In the component named *switch* is a Boolean value, initially switched to *on*. Use of these items is explained later.

The records for edges running out of a node are created dynamically. Each record has a component for storing the link, another for storing

nodefacts[2].head↑.link
nodefacts[2].head↑.tip   5
nodefacts[2].head↑.time   8.0

the node number at the tip, another for storing the journey time along the particular edge. This example is for edge ②→⑤.

The shortest route is found by an iterative process. Before the process can start the chains must be formed and initial values placed in the components that will eventually hold changing values. The component named *bestime* is to hold the best time so far achieved to this node by different trial routes; the initial time in this component is set so high that the first feasible route, however slow, has to be an improvement. An exception is the starting node; the best time to the starting node is, by definition, nothing.

All switches are turned *on* initially. A switch that is *on* implies that the edges leading out of that node must be explored (or re-explored).

The iterative process starts at the starting node, then cycles the array of node records until terminated. The process terminates on detection of all switches being *off*.

At each node the chain of edge records is traversed. For each edge in the chain the time to reach its tip is found by adding the best time so far achieved at the tail to the journey time for that edge. The result is compared with the best time so far recorded in the *node record* for the tip. If the new time is better, several things must be recorded. These are depicted below:

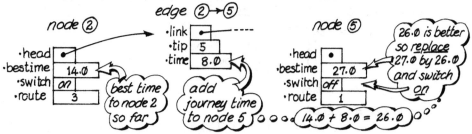

Whenever a better route to a node is found, the faster time is substituted and the node switched *on* as depicted for node 5 above. To be able to trace this improved route subsequently, the *route* component is made to contain the number of the node through which the route came. So the outcome of dealing with the edge from ② to ⑤ is:

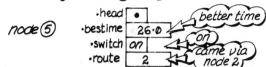

After traversing the chain of edges from node 2 the *switch* at node 2 is turned off. However, the action at node 2 included turning *on* the switch at node 5 so the iteration is not yet finished. The process continues until all switches are off ⇄ in other words until a complete cycle through the nodes fails to make a single improvement to the route.

The node-records are assembled as an array rather than being created dynamically and linked as a chain. The array structure was chosen because node-records are accessed in a "random" way (e.g. when dealing with node 2 you have to refer to nodes 5 and 4). Using an array such references are resolved quickly by a simple change of subscript.

Tried with the network sketched opposite, data and results (assuming interactive use) would be as shown here. ⇨

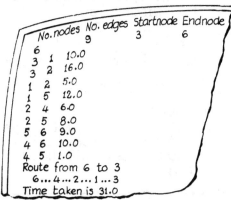

No.nodes	No. edges	Startnode	Endnode
	9	3	6

6		
3	1	10.0
3	2	16.0
1	2	5.0
1	5	12.0
2	4	6.0
2	5	8.0
5	6	9.0
4	6	10.0
4	5	1.0

Route from 6 to 3
6...4...2...1...3
Time taken is 31.0

```pascal
PROGRAM  network ( INPUT, OUTPUT );
  CONST
    on =  TRUE;    off = FALSE;
    huge = 1E20;     nothing = 0.0;
    maxnodes = 30;    maxedges =  50;

  TYPE
    nodetype = 0..maxnodes; edgetype = 0..maxedges;
    pointertype = ↑chaintype;
    chaintype = RECORD
                   link: pointertype;
                   tip: nodetype;
                   time: REAL
                END;

    rectype = RECORD
                 head : pointertype;
                 bestime: REAL;
                 switch: BOOLEAN;
                 route: nodetype
              END;
    arraytype =  ARRAY [nodetype] OF rectype;

  VAR
    nodes, startnode, endnode, i, n, tail : nodetype;
    edges, j : edgetype;
    edge, p: pointertype;
    nodefacts: arraytype;          ←  array of
    cycles: 0..2;   try: REAL;        node records
BEGIN

  WRITELN ( 'No.nodes, No.edges, Startnode, Endnode ');
  READLN ( nodes, edges, startnode, endnode );

  FOR i := 1 TO nodes DO              ←  initialize
    WITH nodefacts[i] DO
      BEGIN
        head := NIL;
        bestime := huge;
        switch := on;
        route := 0                    ←  replace time
      END;          { WITH }             at start node
  nodefacts [startnode].bestime := nothing;

  FOR j := 1 TO edges DO              ←  form all chains
    BEGIN                             ←  read data
      NEW ( p );
      READLN ( tail, p↑.tip, p↑.time );
      p↑.link := nodefacts [tail].head;   ←  link new record
      nodefacts [tail].head := p             to chain
    END;
```

```
      cycles :=  Ø;
      n := startnode - 1;
```
n is augmented by +1 before use, hence -1 in preparation

```
  WHILE   cycles < 2  DO
    BEGIN
       cycles := SUCC( cycles );
       n := n MOD nodes + 1
```
omit the " = on" if you find it clearer

```
      IF  nodefacts[n]. switch = on
        THEN
          BEGIN  { IF switch }
            cycles := Ø;
            edge   := nodefacts [n]. head;

            WHILE  edge <> NIL   DO
              BEGIN    { WHILE edge }
                try := nodefacts[n]. bestime + edge↑.time;
                IF  try < nodefacts [edge↑.tip]. bestime
                  THEN
                    WITH  nodefacts [edge↑.tip] DO
                      BEGIN
                        bestime := try;
                        route := n;
                        switch := on
                      END

                edge := edge↑.link

              END; { WHILE edge }

            nodefacts [n]. switch := off

          END   { IF switch }

    END;   { WHILE cycles }


  WITH  nodefacts [ endnode ]  DO
    IF  (bestime <> huge) AND ( bestime <> nothing )
      THEN
        BEGIN
          WRITELN ('Route from', endnode:3, ' to', startnode:3);
          n := endnode;

          WHILE   n <> Ø  DO
            BEGIN
              WRITE ( n:1 );
              n := nodefacts[n]. route;
              IF n <> Ø THEN  WRITE ('...')
            END;
          WRITELN;
          WRITELN ( 'Time taken is', bestime:6:2)

        END

      ELSE
        WRITELN ('No way through - or going nowhere')
  END.
```
field width expands to 2 if node number has 2 digits

keep looking back to previous node

e.g. 6...4...2...1...3

INTRODUCING RINGS

The fundamental record of a doubly linked ring has pointers pointing fore and aft thus : ▷

Access to records in a ring is simplified by employing one record as a dummy head as illustrated below. This device makes it unnecessary to check whether the record to be added or deleted is next to the fixed head, taking special action accordingly. Very messy.

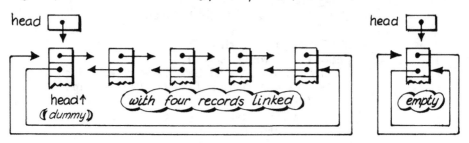

head
head↑
(*dummy*)

with four records linked

head

empty

A ring is depicted above with four records; it is also depicted empty.

Here is the definition of a record suitable for constructing a ring. To keep everything simple this record is made capable of storing just a single character. ▷

```
TYPE
   pointertype = ↑ recordtype;

   recordtype = RECORD
                  fore, aft: pointertype;
                  data : CHAR
                END;
VAR
   head, temp : pointertype;
```

In the main program an empty ring may be set up as follows.

```
NEW ( head );
head↑.fore := head;
head↑.aft := head;
```

A new record may be inserted before *or* after the record currently pointed to. Procedures for both these operations are given below:

```
PROCEDURE  inafter ( old, young : pointertype );
   BEGIN

      young↑. fore := old↑.fore;
      young↑. aft := old;
      old↑.fore↑.aft := young;
      old↑.fore := young

   END;
```

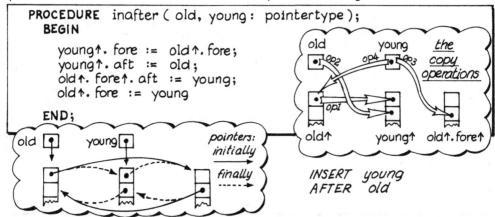

old   young   *the copy operations*

old↑   young↑   old↑.fore↑

old   young

pointers:
initially
finally

INSERT young
AFTER old

150

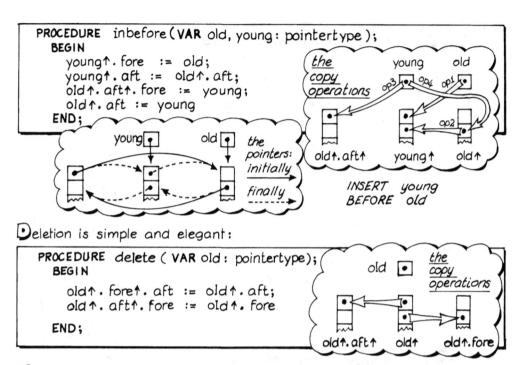

```
PROCEDURE inbefore (VAR old, young: pointertype);
   BEGIN
      young↑. fore  := old;
      young↑. aft  := old↑. aft;
      old↑. aft↑. fore  := young;
      old↑. aft := young
   END;
```

the copy operations

the pointers:
initially
finally

INSERT young BEFORE old

Deletion is simple and elegant:

```
PROCEDURE delete ( VAR old: pointertype);
   BEGIN

      old↑. fore↑. aft  := old↑. aft;
      old ↑. aft↑. fore  := old ↑. fore

   END;
```

the copy operations

Traversal is simple in either direction; the only difficulty is stopping in time. If the aim is to traverse the ring precisely once, start by pointing to the first record and arrange to stop as soon as the pointer points to the dummy head (*before trying to refer to data in the dummy head*).

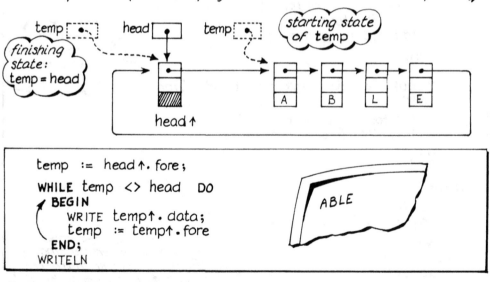

finishing state:
temp = head

starting state of temp

```
temp  := head ↑. fore;

WHILE temp <> head  DO
   BEGIN
      WRITE temp↑. data;
      temp  := temp↑. fore
   END;
WRITELN
```

ABLE

If both occurrences of "fore" were changed to "aft" the result of the above piece of program would be ELBA rather than ABLE.

Overleaf is a demonstration program designed to exercise the principles and procedures introduced on this double page.

AN EXAMPLE PROGRAM TO DEMONSTRATE THE WORKING
OF A DOUBLY-LINKED RING

The following program maintains a doubly-linked ring organized alphabetically. To introduce a letter enter +L (or + any other letter) at the start of a line. To remove a letter enter −L (or − whatever the letter). To display the stored data in alphabetical order enter > at the start of a line. To display in reverse order enter <. To stop enter * at the start of a line.

```
PROGRAM  roses ( INPUT, OUTPUT );
    TYPE

        pointertype = ↑ recordtype;

        recordtype =    RECORD
                            fore, aft : pointertype;
                            data : CHAR
                        END;
    VAR
        ch : CHAR;
        head, p, temp : pointertype;
        caps, operators : SET OF CHAR;

    PROCEDURE   inbefore ( VAR old, young : pointertype );
        BEGIN

            young↑. fore := old;
            young↑. aft := old↑. aft ;
            old↑. aft↑. fore :=  young ;
            old↑. aft := young

        END;

    PROCEDURE  delete ( VAR old : pointertype );
        BEGIN

            old↑. fore↑. aft := old↑. aft ;
            old↑. aft↑. fore := old↑. fore

        END;

BEGIN
    caps :=  ['A'..'z'];
    operators := [ '+', '-', '>', '<' ];

    NEW ( head );
    head↑. fore  := head;
    head↑. aft   := head;
    head↑. data  := CHR ( 0 );
    REPEAT

        READ ( ch );
        IF ch IN operators
            THEN
```

> procedures inbefore and delete as on previous page

> set up an empty ring. put a dummy character CHR(0) into dummy head to avoid the crash warned about on the next page

Note panel (right margin):
```
+R
+O
>
OR
+S
+E
+S
>
EORSS
-S
<
SROE
*
```

```
    CASE  ch  OF

      '+' :  BEGIN
                READ ( ch );
                IF ch   IN  caps
                  THEN
                    BEGIN
                      NEW( p );
                      p↑. data := ch;
                      temp := head↑. fore;
                      WHILE (temp<>head) AND (temp↑. data< ch) DO
                         temp := temp↑. fore;
                      inbefore ( temp, p )
                    END
             END;

      '-' :  BEGIN
                READ ( ch );
                IF ch   IN  caps
                  THEN
                    BEGIN
                      temp := head↑. fore;
                      WHILE (temp<>head) AND (temp↑. data <>ch)  DO
                         temp := temp↑. fore;
                      IF  temp <> head
                        THEN
                          delete( temp )
                    END
             END;

      '>' :  BEGIN
                temp := head↑. fore;
                WHILE  temp <> head   DO
                  BEGIN
                     WRITE ( temp↑. data );
                     temp := temp↑. fore
                  END;
                WRITELN
             END;

      '<' :  BEGIN
                temp := head↑. aft;
                WHILE  temp <> head   DO
                  BEGIN
                     WRITE ( temp↑. data );
                     temp := temp↑. aft
                  END;
                WRITELN
             END
    END { CASE }

  UNTIL  ch = '*'

END.  { roses }
```

Beware of a potential crash. The condition temp↑. data < ch will be evaluated even when the condition temp<>head is false. So temp↑. data must not be left undefined in the dummy head. Hence the CHR(0)

insert

delete

display in ascending order

display in descending order

stop work on *

INTRODUCING BINARY TREES

ANOTHER ELEGANCE

Take some letters to sort:

D, Z, B, E, A, F, C

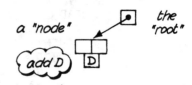

a "node"   the "root"

Bring the first letter, D, to the root of a *tree* and store it in a *node*. (Trees grow upside down as do several metaphors in computer science.)

add D D

Now take the next letter, Z, and bring it to the root node. It is "bigger" than D so go *right* and make a new node to contain Z as shown ⟵ here.

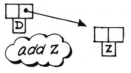

add Z

Now the third letter, B. It is smaller than D so go *left* and make a new node. ↗ *add B*

The next letter, E, is bigger than D so go *right*. It is smaller than Z so go *left*. Then make a new node to contain E as shown here.

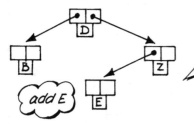

add E

In general; bring the next letter to the root node and compare. If the new letter is smaller go *left*, if bigger go *right*. Do the same thing as you reach each node until there are no more nodes to supply letters for comparison. Then make a new node to contain the new letter.

add A

add F

add C

At any stage the tree may be traversed (or *stripped*) as shown below. Notice that the arrow runs through the letters in alphabetical order. ✽

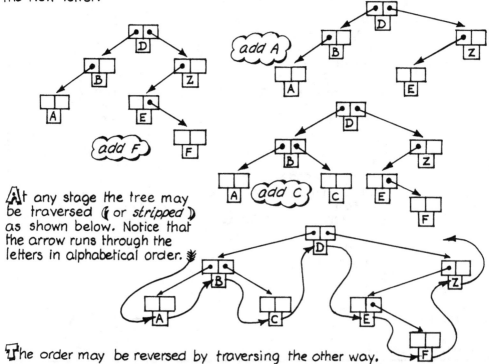

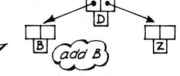

The order may be reversed by traversing the other way.

154

The type of node record depicted opposite is easily defined:

```
TYPE
    pointertype = ↑ nodetype;                    ·left ☐☐ ·right
                                                  ·data
    nodetype = RECORD
                 left, right : pointertype;
                 data :   CHAR
               END;
```

Hanging letters on a tree ⇋ depicted in stages opposite ⇋ is best done
recursively. If the current node is NIL make a new node to contain the new
letter; otherwise invoke the "hang" procedure with the parameter specifying the
left or right pointer according to how the new letter compares with that pointed to:

```
PROCEDURE  hang( VAR nptr : pointertype;  ch: CHAR );
  BEGIN
    IF   nptr = NIL
      THEN     { CASE 1 }
        BEGIN
          NEW ( nptr );
          nptr↑.left   :=  NIL;
          nptr↑.right  :=  NIL;
          nptr↑.data   :=  ch
        END
      ELSE     { CASE 2 }
      IF ch <  nptr↑.data
        THEN  hang( nptr↑.left, ch)
        ELSE IF  ch >  nptr↑.data
            THEN   hang ( nptr↑.right, ch)
            ELSE   WRITELN ('Duplicate entry')
  END;
```

VAR essential: nptr changed by NEW (nptr)

CASE 1 — nptr NIL ... nptr ● ... NIL NIL / ch → NEW

CASE 2 — nptr ● ... nptr↑.left ●● nptr↑.right / ? nptr↑.data

The tree may be traversed recursively :

```
PROCEDURE  strip ( VAR nptr : pointertype );
  BEGIN
    IF   nptr <> NIL
      THEN
        BEGIN
          strip ( nptr↑.left );
          WRITE ( nptr↑.data );
          strip ( nptr↑.right )
        END
  END;
```

strip the left subtree
then deal with the node
then strip the right subtree
isn't this pretty?

In both the above procedures " WITH nptr↑ DO" could be used to reduce the
number of occurrences of "nptr↑" at the cost of extra lines and less clarity.
The VAR in the traversal procedure, though not logically necessary, prevents
the processor taking a copy of the data structure on each invocation. Ouch!

Over the page is a program based on a binary tree. It reads letters typed
in any order and displays them in alphabetical order. It is left as an
exercise to add a facility for display in reverse order.

Binary trees are useful for all sorts of things besides sorting.

MONKEY~PUZZLE SORT
ANOTHER NAME FOR BINARY-TREE SORT

This program maintains a binary tree in much the same way as Roses maintains a doubly-linked ring. To hang a new letter on the tree enter +L (or + any letter). To remove a letter enter −L (or minus whatever the letter). To display the letters on the tree in alphabetical order enter > at the start of a line. Enter * at the start of a line to stop.

Adding to the tree is elegantly simple but deleting a node which is not a "leaf" ⇆ especially when duplicated items are allowed on the tree ⇆ is not easy at all. This program simply keeps a count of like items, reducing the count when an item is deleted.

```
PROGRAM monkey( INPUT, OUTPUT );

  TYPE
    pointertype = ↑ nodetype;

    nodetype = RECORD
                 left, right: pointertype;
                 data: CHAR;
                 count: INTEGER
               END;

  VAR
    root, p: pointertype;
    ch : CHAR;

  PROCEDURE hang( VAR nptr: pointertype;  ch: CHAR );
    BEGIN
      IF nptr = NIL
        THEN
          BEGIN
            NEW( nptr );
            nptr↑.left   := NIL;
            nptr↑.right  := NIL;
            nptr↑.data   := ch;
            nptr↑.count  := 1
          END
        ELSE
          IF  ch < nptr↑.data
            THEN
              hang( nptr↑.left, ch )
            ELSE IF ch > nptr↑.data
                    THEN
                      hang( nptr↑.right, ch )
                    ELSE
                      nptr↑.count := nptr↑.count + 1
    END;
```

augment the count if a duplicate

Side note (receipt paper):
```
+B
+A
+B
+O
+O
+N
>
ABBNOO
-B
>
ABNOO
*
```

The following function is for finding a letter to be deleted. The function is written recursively using the same logic as in *hang*.

```
    FUNCTION  find (VAR nptr: pointertype; ch: CHAR): pointertype;
      BEGIN
        IF   nptr = NIL
           THEN   find := NIL          return NIL
           ELSE IF  ch < nptr↑.data    if not found
                   THEN   find := find (nptr↑.left, ch)
                   ELSE IF  ch > nptr↑.data
                           THEN   find := find ( nptr↑.right, ch)
                           ELSE   find := nptr           found
      END;                                                it

    PROCEDURE  strip ( VAR nptr: pointertype);
      VAR
        i :  0 .. MAXINT;
      BEGIN
        IF  nptr <> NIL
          THEN
            BEGIN
              strip ( nptr↑. left );                e.g. if the count
              FOR i := 1 TO nptr↑.count  DO         is 2 write the letter
                WRITE ( nptr↑.data);                twice; if the count
              strip ( nptr↑. right )                is 0 don't write
            END                                     anything
      END;

BEGIN  { monkey }
  root := NIL;
  REPEAT
    READ( ch );
    IF  ch  IN  ['+','-','>']
      THEN
        CASE  ch  OF
        '+':  BEGIN
                READ ( ch );
                IF  ch  IN   ['A' .. 'z']
                    THEN
                      hang ( root, ch )
              END;

        '-':  BEGIN
                READ( ch );
                p := find ( root, ch );
                IF p <> NIL
                    THEN IF p↑.count > 0
                            THEN p↑.count := p↑.count - 1
              END;
                                              effectively delete
        '>':  BEGIN                           one copy of
                strip ( root );               letter
                WRITELN
              END
        END    { CASE }
  UNTIL ch = '*'
END.
```

EXERCISES

1. Write a program to read an arithmetic expression such as:

$$3.5 * (7 + (4 - 6.2) / 32)$$

and display the answer. Use an input procedure such as *grab* (pages 118-23) to read the numbers and operators which comprise the expression. Employ the logic of the reverse Polish program (pages 142-4) but with an important difference; when you are about to transfer an operator from stack Y to stack X do the following instead:

- pop two numbers from stack X
- apply the operator to them
- push the result on stack X

By this device you should end up with a single number in stack X; this is the value of the expression.

2. Write an adventure game. The player explores a mystic palace or smelly dungeon, walking from room to room, picking things up, putting things down, whilst contending with monsters. To write such a program you need the string-handling facilities developed in the next chapter because the player expects to type:

    TAKE POISON
or
    GO WEST

and have the computer respond intelligently. There is a simple but complete adventure game described in my book:

Illustrating Super-BASIC   C.U.P. 1985

which exploits ring structures for picking things up in one room and dropping them in another, state matrices for mapping the topology of rooms and doors, and symbol-state tables for encoding the rules of play. Enough techniques are described for constructing a complete and worthwhile adventure game.

13

DYNAMIC STRINGS

STRING UTILITIES

- READSTRING
- WRITESTRING
- MIDDLE
- CONCAT
- COMPARE
- INSTR
- PEEK
- POKE

BACKSLANG (EXAMPLE)
HASHING TECHNIQUE
HASHER (EXAMPLE)

STRING UTILITIES
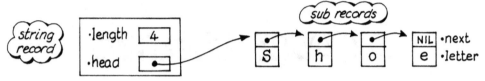

Standard Pascal defines few string-handling facilities; as a consequence modern compilers offer non-standard ones. The disadvantage of using non-standard facilities is loss of portability. One way round the portability problem is to define one's own set of utilities built strictly from standard parts. This course is followed below. Its purpose is to suggest and illustrate a methodical approach rather than attempt the standardization of string utilities; the reader is sure to want different facilities and better written procedures than those to be found here.

The utilities are based on a record of the form depicted below:

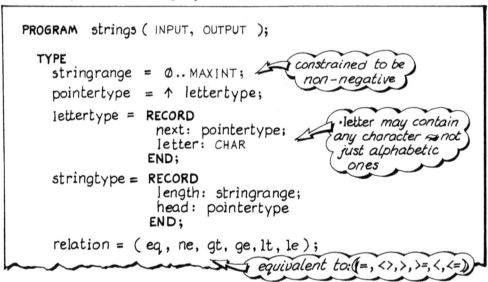

Because dynamic storage is employed every string may have a different length and there is no arbitrary limit placed on length. Here is the type definition. (Also included is a definition of enumerated type for later use in the comparison of strings.)

```
PROGRAM  strings ( INPUT, OUTPUT );

   TYPE
      stringrange  = 0.. MAXINT;         constrained to be
      pointertype  = ↑ lettertype;       non-negative

      lettertype = RECORD
                     next: pointertype;       ·letter may contain
                     letter: CHAR             any character ≈ not
                   END;                       just alphabetic
                                              ones
      stringtype = RECORD
                     length: stringrange;
                     head: pointertype
                   END;

      relation = ( eq, ne, gt, ge, lt, le );
                          equivalent to:( =, <>, >, >=, <, <= )
```

The first two procedures are recursive. *Append* is for appending a new character to the end of a string; *reclaim* is for disposing of subrecords when a record is to store a new string. These are "low-level" procedures used by the main string utilities. The programmer who uses the main string utilities need not know about the low-level ones.

Throughout all procedures the parameters which nominate string records are made VAR parameters. The idea is to prevent the processor having to make copies of strings ≈ which could be very long.

```
PROCEDURE append ( VAR p: pointertype;  c: CHAR );
  BEGIN
    IF  p = NIL
      THEN
        BEGIN
          NEW( p );
          p↑.letter := c;
          p↑.next := NIL
        END
      ELSE
        append ( p↑.next, c )
  END;


PROCEDURE  reclaim ( VAR p: pointertype );
  BEGIN
    IF  p <> NIL
      THEN
        BEGIN
          IF  p↑.next <> NIL
            THEN
              reclaim ( p↑.next );

          DISPOSE ( p );
          p := NIL
        END
  END;
```

recursion

recursion

Assume a string named *st* :

VAR st : stringtype;

st.length [2]
st.head [•] → [• | 0] → [NIL | h]

The effect of *append(st.head, '!')* would be:

not updated by append →
st.length [2]
st.head [•] → [• | 0] → [• | h] → [NIL | !]

The effect of *reclaim(st.head)* would be:

not made zero →
st.length [2]
st.head [NIL]

the heap

The following depicts an *empty* string. Before any string is used by name in the procedures that follow, that string must be initialized. You could write a formal procedure to do this but it's not worth the effort and complication.

st.head := NIL ;
st.length := 0

st.length [0]
st.head [NIL]

THIS IS HOW TO INITIALIZE

THIS IS THE EMPTY STRING DEPICTED

READSTRING (*name* ~string~)   *CHECK EOLN BEFORE INVOCATION*

The following procedure reads a string and stores it under the specified name. The specified name may be the name of an empty string or of a non-empty string, the previous content being lost. It is an error to invoke the procedure with the name of a string not yet initialized. A string is considered terminated by a *space* or *EOLN* (*i.e.* the RETURN key pressed). Leading spaces are ignored by this procedure.

```
PROCEDURE  readstring ( VAR newstring: stringtype);
  CONST
    space = ' ';
  VAR
    ch: CHAR;
  BEGIN
    reclaim( newstring.head );
    newstring.length := 0;
    REPEAT
      READ( ch )
    UNTIL  ( ch <> space) OR  EOLN;
    IF  ch <> space
      THEN
        REPEAT
          append( newstring.head, ch );
          newstring.length := newstring.length + 1;
          ch := space;
          IF NOT EOLN THEN  READ( ch )
        UNTIL  ch = space
  END;
```

reclaim does nothing if newstring is already empty

ignore leading spaces

count characters

WRITESTRING (*name* ~string~)   *DOES NOTHING WITH AN EMPTY STRING*

The following procedure writes a copy of the nominated string with no leading spaces and no trailing spaces or new-line characters. If the nominated string is empty the procedure does nothing.

```
PROCEDURE  writestring ( VAR oldstring: stringtype);
  VAR
    p: pointertype;
  BEGIN
    p := oldstring.head;
    WHILE   p <> NIL DO
      BEGIN
        WRITE ( p↑.letter );
        p := p↑.next
      END
  END;
```

MIDDLE ($name_{newstring}$, $name_{oldstring}$, $start_{position}$, $span_{no.\ of\ chars}$)

This procedure creates a string by copying part of another. The new string is made a copy of the "middle" of the old string starting at a specified position and having a specified number of characters. Use of parameters is best explained pictorially:

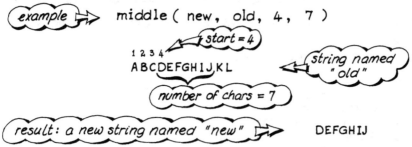

example ⇒ middle (new, old, 4, 7)

start = 4

1 2 3 4
ABCDEFGHIJKL

string named "old"

number of chars = 7

result: a new string named "new" ⇒ DEFGHIJ

This procedure is modelled on the popular *BASIC* command *MID$*(, ,).

The fourth parameter may specify an impossibly high value, in which case the new string is truncated where the old string ends. The procedure may be used to copy a complete string. A new string may be made to overwrite the old string.

```
PROCEDURE  middle ( VAR newstring, oldstring : stringtype;
                         start, span : stringrange );
   VAR
      i : stringrange;   p, temp : pointertype;

   BEGIN
      IF  (start > 0)  AND  (start <= oldstring.length)
         THEN
            BEGIN
               temp := NIL;
               p := oldstring.head;              run as far
               i := 1;                           as "start"
               WHILE   i < start  DO
                  BEGIN
                     p := p↑.next;
                     i := SUCC( i )              truncate if
                  END;                           "span" is too big
               i := 1;
               WHILE  ( p <> NIL) AND ( i <= span) DO
                  BEGIN
                     append ( temp, p↑.letter );
                     p := p↑.next;               build result
                     i := i + 1                  as a temporary
                  END;                           string
               newstring.length := i - 1;
               reclaim ( newstring.head );       reclaim space,
               newstring.head := temp            then point to
            END                                  "temporary"
   END;                                          string
```

163

CONCAT ($name_{newstring}$ **,** $name_{leftstring}$ **,** $name_{rightstring}$ **)**

This procedure creates a new string as a copy of two nominated strings joined end to end ~ in other words concatenated. The left and right strings nominated for concatenation remain undisturbed unless the new string is to overwrite one of them.

```
PROCEDURE  concat ( VAR newstring, left, right:  stringtype);
    VAR
        p, temp:  pointertype;
    BEGIN
        temp := NIL;
        p := left.head;
        WHILE p <> NIL  DO
            BEGIN
                append( temp,  p↑.letter );
                p := p↑.next
            END;

        p := right.head;
        WHILE p <> NIL  DO
            BEGIN
                append( temp, p↑.letter );
                p := p↑.next
            END;
        newstring.length := left.length + right.length;
        reclaim ( newstring.head );
        newstring.head := temp
    END;
```

The next function is for comparing strings. The criteria for equality and relative size are those commonly used for alphabetical directories. Upper case letters are considered "equal" to corresponding lower-case letters. Strings are "equal" if they have identical length and all characters match in pairs from left to right:

$$AbCd \text{ is considered "equal" to } aBCd$$

When strings are *unequal* their relative order in a directory is determined by the first mismatching character from the left. The one with the higher ordinal value indicates the greater string:

AbCdg *is considered "greater than"* aBCdefg
first mismatching character

When one string is shorter than another imagine a "null" character of zero ordinal value appended to the shorter. The rule above then still applies:

AbCde *is considered "greater than"* aBC *imaginary "null"*
first mismatching character

164

criterion for returning true:
eq , ne, gt, ge, lt, le
$= , <>, > , >=, <, <=$

examples: IF compare(response, eq , affirm) THEN ...
IF compare(left, ge, right) THEN ...

enumerated
on page 160

```
FUNCTION compare ( VAR left: stringtype; r: relation;
                        VAR right: stringtype ): BOOLEAN;
   VAR
      cp, cq: CHAR;
      same, pmore, qmore : BOOLEAN;
      p, q : pointertype;

   FUNCTION upper ( c: CHAR ): CHAR;
      BEGIN
         IF c IN [ 'a' .. 'z' ]
            THEN
               upper := CHR( ORD(c) - ORD('a') + ORD('A'))
            ELSE
               upper := c
      END;

   BEGIN  { compare }

      p := left.head;      q := right.head;
      pmore := p <> NIL; qmore := q <> NIL;
      same := TRUE;
      WHILE ( pmore AND qmore ) AND same DO
         BEGIN
            cp := upper( p↑.letter );
            cq := upper( q↑.letter );
            same := cp=cq ;
            p := p↑.next; pmore := p <> NIL;
            q := q↑.next; qmore := q <> NIL
         END;

      IF ( same AND qmore ) AND ( NOT pmore )
         THEN cp := CHR( 0 );
      IF ( same AND pmore ) AND ( NOT qmore )
         THEN cq := CHR( 0 );

      CASE r  OF

         eq : compare :=    cp = cq;
         ne : compare :=    cp <> cq;
         gt : compare :=    cp > cq;
         ge : compare :=    cp >= cq;
         lt : compare :=    cp < cq;
         le : compare :=    cp <= cq

      END   { CASE }
   END;  { compare }
```

when comparing strings any lower-case letter is treated as a capital letter

assume this offset is constant: from a → z A → Z

CHR(0) is bound to be less than any character it is compared with

This function is modelled on a popular function of *BASIC*. It seeks the first occurrence of *substring* within *superstring*, returning its position as an integer counting from 1 ⇌ or zero if no match is found.

example superstring ⇨ $\overset{1\,2\,3}{A\,b\,c\,d\,a\,B\,c\,D}$ ⇇ function returns 3

substring ⇨ c D ⇇ does not find subsequent match

```
FUNCTION instr ( VAR super, sub: stringtype ): stringrange ;
VAR
    tempstring:  stringtype;
    i, j: stringrange;
    match : BOOLEAN
BEGIN
    instr := 0;
    tempstring.head := NIL;
    i := 0;
    j := super.length - sub.length + 1;
    IF   j >= 1
        THEN
            BEGIN
                REPEAT
                    i := SUCC( i );                    take a short temporary
                    middle( tempstring, super, i, sub.length );   string from successive positions
                    match := compare ( tempstring, eq , sub )        in super
                UNTIL match OR ( i = j );
                IF match THEN instr := i;              compare the temporary
                reclaim ( tempstring.head )            string with sub
            END
    END;
```

───

PEEK (($name_{string}$, $n_{position}$)) **FUNCTION RETURNS** n^{th} **CHARACTER**

This function returns the character at position *n* of the nominated string, or CHR(0) if *n* is beyond the range of that string.

```
FUNCTION peek ( VAR old: stringtype;  n: stringrange ): CHAR;
VAR
    i: stringrange;   p: pointertype;
BEGIN                                          str ⇨ $\overset{1\,2}{ABCD}$
    p := old.head;
    i := 1;                                        peek( str, 2)
    WHILE ( i < n ) AND ( p <> NIL ) DO            returns 'B'
        BEGIN
            i := SUCC ( i );
            p := p↑.next                           EXAMPLE
        END;
    IF p <> NIL
        THEN
            peek := p↑.letter              position given
        ELSE                               outside range
            peek := CHR( 0 )               of string
END;
```

POKE ($name_{string}$, $n_{position}$, $c_{character}$) **REPLACES** n^{th} **CHARACTER WITH c**

This procedure is versatile:

- when $1 \leqslant n \leqslant length$ the procedure replaces the nth character of the nominated string with the given character:

    $str \Rightarrow$ asKa   POKE (str, 3, 'c') $str \Rightarrow$ asca

- when $n = \emptyset$ the given character is pushed on the front:

    $str \Rightarrow$ asca   POKE (str, $\emptyset$, 'P') $str \Rightarrow$ Pasca

- when $n > length$ the given character is appended:

    $str \Rightarrow$ Pasca   POKE (str, 6, 'l') $str \Rightarrow$ Pascal

String "constants" may be built from empty strings in this manner. For long string constants it would be better to write a procedure to build strings from Pascal string constants assigned to packed arrays of characters.

```
PROCEDURE poke ( VAR old: stringtype; n: stringrange; c: CHAR;
   VAR
     p: pointertype;
     i: stringrange;

   BEGIN
     IF  n > old.length
       THEN
         BEGIN                                    n > length ;
           append ( old.head, c );                append
           old.length := old.length + 1
         END
       ELSE IF n = 0
              THEN                                 n = 0 ;
                BEGIN                              push on front
                  NEW ( p );
                  p↑.next := old.head;
                  p↑.letter := c;
                  old.head := p;
                  old.length := old.length + 1
                END
              ELSE                                 1 ≤ n ≤ length;
                BEGIN                              replace n th
                  p := old.head;                     character
                  i := 1;
                  WHILE  ( i < n ) AND ( p <> NIL )  DO
                    BEGIN
                      i := SUCC ( i );
                      p := p↑.next
                    END;
                  IF  p <> NIL
                    THEN
                      p↑.letter := c
                END
   END;
```

BACK~SLANG

Isthay isay Ackslangbay! Ancay ouyay eadray itay? Erhapspay otnay atay irstfay.

Backslang is a secret language spoken in boarding schools. It is suitably incomprehensible when heard for the first time but easy to master once you know the grammatical rules. There are probably many dialects of backslang (also called *pig Latin*); this one is remembered from school days. Each English word is folded about its first vowel and *ay* is appended (*tea → eatay, tomato → omatotay*). If a word begins with a vowel, the second vowel becomes the pivot (*item → emitay*) unless there is no second vowel in which case there is no fold (*itch → itchay*). A diphthong at the beginning of a word is treated as a single vowel (*oil → oilay* not *iloay*; *earwig → igearway* not *arwigeay*).

A capital letter at the beginning of a word has to be transformed (*Godfather → Odfathergay* not *odfatherGay*). The *u* after *q* demands special treatment (*Queen → Eenquay* not *ueenQay*). A trailing punctuation mark has to remain trailing (*Crumbs! → Umbscray!* not *Umbs!cray*).

To make all this work properly the input file for the following program should be typed without pressing the RETURN key until the end. Type in lower-case but capitalize words wherever appropriate. There should be a space after ⇄ and not before ⇄ each punctuation mark. Quotation marks, double or single, are not catered for so should be omitted; embedded punctuation marks such as apostrophes are treated as consonants.

Try the following input file which should make the program encipher and display the text shown at the very top of this page:

> This is Backslang! Can you read it? Perhaps not at first.

```
PROCEDURE colossus;
   VAR
      puncmark: CHAR;
      recap: BOOLEAN;
      btm: 2..3;
      fold, k, quin: stringrange;
      offset: INTEGER;
      word, fore, aft, qu, ay,: stringtype;

   BEGIN

      word.head := NIL;   word.length := 0;
      fore.head := NIL;   fore.length := 0;
      aft.head := NIL;    aft.length := 0;
      ay.head := NIL;     ay.length := 0;
      qu.head := NIL;     qu.length := 0;

      offset := ORD('a') - ORD('A');

      poke(ay,1,'a'); poke(ay,2,'y'); poke(ay,3,' ');
      poke(qu,0,'u'); poke(qu,0,'q');
```

(the real purpose of this example is to show how to apply the string facilities developed on earlier pages)

initialize all string variables

"string constants" 'ay' and 'qu'

space

```
        WHILE NOT EOLN DO
          BEGIN
            readstring( word );
            recap := peek( word, 1 ) IN [ 'A'..'Z' ];
            IF recap
              THEN
                poke( word, 1, CHR( ORD( peek( word, 1 )) + offset ));
            IF NOT  ( peek( word, word.length) IN  [ 'A'..'Z', 'a'..'z' ] )
              THEN
                BEGIN
                  puncmark :=  peek( word, word.length );
                  IF word.length = 1
                    THEN
                      poke( word, 0, ' ' );
                  middle( word, word, 1, word.length - 1 )
                END
              ELSE
                puncmark := CHR( 0 );
            quin := instr( word, qu );
            IF quin > 0
              THEN
                poke( word, quin+1, '*' );
            IF peek( word, 1 ) IN [ 'A','a','E','e','I','i','O','o','U','u' ]
              THEN btm := 3
              ELSE btm := 2;
            fold := 1;
            FOR  k := word.length DOWNTO btm DO
              IF peek( word, k ) IN [ 'A','a','E','e','I','i','O','o','U','u' ]
                THEN
                  fold := k;
            IF quin > 0
              THEN
                poke( word, quin+1, 'u' );
            middle( fore, word, fold, word.length - fold + 1 );
            middle( aft, word, 1, fold - 1 );
            concat( word, fore, aft );
            concat( word, word, ay );
            IF puncmark <> CHR( 0 )
              THEN
                BEGIN
                  poke( word, word.length, puncmark );
                  poke( word, 1 + word.length, ' ' )
                END;
            IF recap AND ( peek( word, 1 ) IN [ 'a'..'z' ] )
              THEN
                poke( word, 1, CHR( ORD( peek( word, 1 )) - offset ));
            writestring( word )
          END;  { WHILE }
        WRITELN
    END;  { colossus }

BEGIN   { strings }
  colossus
END.    { strings }
```

Annotations (in hand-written clouds):
- *if initial letter is a capital, reduce to l/c*
- *if last character is not a letter remember it as a punctuation mark*
- *if word contains 'qu' change to 'q*'*
- *gear or earwig* / *btm = 2 or btm = 3*
- *restore 'u' after 'q'*
- *fold word; append 'ay'*
- *append punctuation mark if there was one*
- *recapitalize if necessary*
- *the main program*

HASHING TECHNIQUE FOR LOOKING THINGS UP QUICKLY

How do you locate a word in a list of words? The simplest solution is to scan the list from top to bottom, arranging to do something when a match is found. Here is a trivial piece of program to locate the letter 'c' in a list of letters. There is nothing wrong with such an approach provided that the list of words is short.

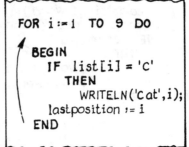

```
FOR i := 1 TO 9 DO

  BEGIN
    IF list[i] = 'c'
      THEN
        WRITELN('Cat',i);
    lastposition := i
  END
```

list[1]	'P'
list[2]	'O'
list[3]	'L'
list[4]	'I'
list[5]	'C'
list[6]	'E'
list[7]	'M'
list[8]	'A'
list[9]	'N'

In long lists the trick is to go straight to the place where the match ought to be found. In a list of letters having a length of 26 the technique would be perfect; such a list would be arranged in alphabetical order, so to find if 'c' is there you would look in list[3]. To find any letter x you would look in list[ORD(x) - ORD('A') + 1]. The expression ORD(x)–ORD('A') +1 in mathematical terminology is a *function* of x. This function returns the correct address for any letter x.

But it would be impractical to provide a list of *words* in which every conceivable word had an exclusive address. The practical solution is to set a limit to the length of list and devise a function (similar to the one illustrated above) to give the *probable* address of the word sought. Such a function is called a *hash function*.

A hash function looks and behaves like a function for generating random numbers. Just as a random-number function involves the use of MOD to constrain the result to a particular range, so does a hash function employ MOD to constrain the address to lie within the length of list. The hash function shown below is based on one given by Kernighan and Plauger†.

Take the word ANT which is to find its place in a list of 17 components, 0 to 16. Ordinal values of the letters are used in the hash function; those below are in ASCII code but the method would work on computers with other codes.

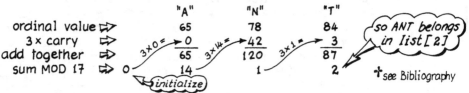

	"A"	"N"	"T"	
ordinal value ⇨	65	78	84	so ANT belongs in list[2]
3 × carry ⇨	3×0= 0	3×14= 42	3×1= 3	
add together ⇨	65	120	87	
sum MOD 17 ⇨ 0	14	1	2	†see Bibliography

(initialize)

By the same algorithm AARDVARK would generate a hash code of 7 and so belong in list[7]. From the addresses of ANT and AARDVARK it is evident that hash codes do not arrange words in alphabetical order. Hashing STOAT yields a hash code of 2 in competition with ANT. Clashes such as this are resolved by the logic explained opposite.

The 3 is a "magic number"; you could try 5 or 7 or other small prime. The length of list (17 in the example) should also be a prime number for best effect. "Best" means distributing the hash codes evenly over the list so that it is not filled in clumps. On page 172 is a program to demonstrate the hash function described above; try it to see if you get clumping (I don't).

To put a new word into a list:

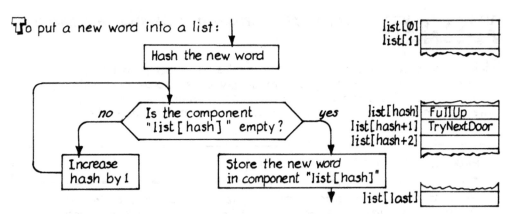

The list should be made "circular" so that when *hash* reaches *last* an increase of 1 makes *hash* revert to zero. There should also be a mechanism to stop the search going round indefinitely when the list is full.

To locate a word:

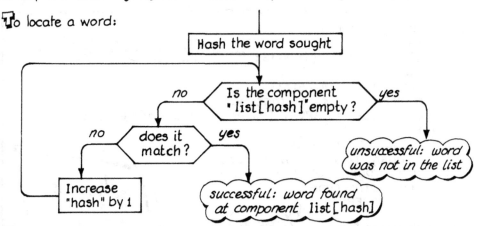

The program over the page is designed to demonstrate the effect of hashing. To use it, simply enter words. Each "new" word is stored in the list and the list displayed in full, showing where the word is stored. When an "old" word is found its location is reported. The program initially assumes that a given word is "old" and goes searching for it. If the search proves unsuccessful the program stores the given word as a "new" one.

The program relies upon the string utilities developed earlier ≈ thus capital letters are treated as equal to corresponding lower-case letters: ANT ≡ Ant.

The data structure comprises an array of pointers pointing to records of *stringtype*. The array of pointers has to be dimensioned and initialized but the rest of the data are created dynamically.

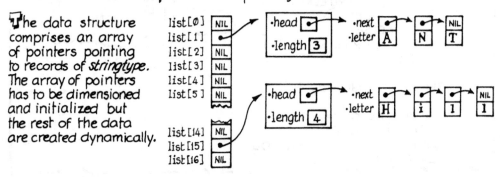

171

Here is the program based on the principles introduced on the previous double page. To use the program simply enter words and watch the screen to see where the words are stored. Enter some words previously entered and notice that duplicate copies are not stored; their location is reported instead.

```
PROGRAM hasher ( INPUT, OUTPUT );
```

include here the declarations and utilities employed in the strings program on pages 160-7 (i.e. omit procedure colossus and the main program on pages 168-9). Procedures middle, concat, instr and poke are not invoked by the hashing procedure so may also be omitted if desired.

```
PROCEDURE hashplay;
  CONST
    size = 17;    siz = 16;        ⟵ keep one less than size
  TYPE
    sizerange = 0 .. siz;
    nametype = ↑ stringtype;
    arraytype = ARRAY [ sizerange ] OF nametype;
  VAR
    name: stringtype;
    i, hash, recall : sizerange;
    full, found, ahole : BOOLEAN;
    list : arraytype;
    n : INTEGER;

  PROCEDURE show;        show on screen
    VAR
      i : sizerange;
    BEGIN
      FOR i := 0 TO siz DO
        IF list [ i ] <> NIL
          THEN                   2 spaces
            BEGIN
              WRITE ( i, '  ' );
              writestring ( list [ i ]↑ );
              WRITELN
            END
          ELSE                1 space
            WRITELN ( i, ' *' )
    END;

  BEGIN   { hashplay }

    name.head := NIL;
    full := FALSE;
    FOR i := 0 TO siz DO
      list [ i ] := NIL;
```

Hill
Stored at 15
```
 0    *
 1    *
 2      ANT
 3    *
 4    *
 5    *
 6    *
 7    *
 8    *
 9    *
10    *
11    *
12    *
13    *
14    *
15      Hill
16    *
```

```
        REPEAT
          readstring ( name );
          hash := 0;
          FOR   i := 1  TO  name.length  DO
            BEGIN
              n := ORD( peek ( name , i ) );
              IF n  IN  [ ORD('a') .. ORD ('z') ]
                THEN
                  n := n - ORD('a') + ORD('A');
              hash := ( 3 * hash + n ) MOD size
            END;
          ahole := list[hash] = NIL;
          IF NOT ahole
            THEN
              BEGIN
                recall := hash;
                REPEAT
                  found := compare( name, eq, list [ hash ]↑ );
                  IF found
                    THEN
                      WRITELN ( 'Found at', hash:4)
                    ELSE
                      BEGIN
                        hash := ( 1 + hash ) MOD size;
                        ahole := list [ hash ] = NIL;
                        full := hash = recall
                      END
                UNTIL ( ahole  OR  found ) OR  full
              END;

          IF ahole
            THEN
              BEGIN
                NEW ( list [ hash ] );
                list [ hash ]↑ := name;
                WRITELN ( 'Stored at', hash : 3 );
                WRITELN;
                show;
                name.head := NIL
              END
            ELSE IF full
                    THEN
                      BEGIN
                        WRITELN ( 'List full');
                        show
                      END
        UNTIL full
      END;  { hashplay }


BEGIN   {main program }
  hashplay
END.   {main program }
```

change lower-case to capital for comparing

the hashing function

augment hash by 1

list[hash] ·head ·length

copy

·head ·length 3 A N T name

important! failure to do this would allow readstring to dispose of the word that name still points to

BIBLIOGRAPHY

BSI Specification for *Computer programming language Pascal*   BS6192: 1982

The British Standard defines the dialect of Pascal presented in my book. BS6192 is not bed-time reading but if you are looking for precise syntax or the defined behaviour of a Pascal processor under rare circumstances then BS6192 is what you need. Its preface tries to explain a complicated relationship between BS6192 and ISO 7185 but I have not yet deciphered it. Apparently BS6192 and ISO 7185 were supposed to be the same but aren't quite.

Jensen, K. & Wirth, N. (1975). *Pascal user manual and report.* (Springer-Verlag)

This was the first book on Pascal; this book's co-author, Niklaus Wirth, being the inventor of the language. The user manual by Kathleen Jensen is a model of conciseness and makes fine historical reading.

Grogono, Peter (1980). *Programming in PASCAL* (Addison-Wesley)

This is the classic; first published in 1978 with word-processed text but now nicely type-set. It is still the best book I have seen for a full course on programming in Pascal. The writing is clear and the examples imaginative. To get the best from the book you have to work hard and get stuck into the long examples. Grogono gives a long and authoritative bibliography for the reader who wants to dig deeper still.

Brown, P. J. (1982). *Pascal from BASIC*   (Addison-Wesley)

A good self-teach book, easy to understand yet does not dodge awkward issues. Strange characters like Prof. Primple 《 archetypal academic 》 and Bill Mudd 《 enthusiastic bodger 》 keep appearing to emphasize different attitudes to programming but one learns to forgive their intrusion. Advanced data structures and dynamic storage are dealt with briefly. This book should help the erstwhile BASIC enthusiast to switch allegiance to Pascal and clean habits.

Kernighan, B.W. & Plauger, P.J. (1981). *Software tools in Pascal* (Addison-Wesley)

A book full of tested and practical applications of Pascal. The sentence: "A picture is worth about a thousand words" appears next to one of only two pictures in the whole book; the rest is 95,000 words of text. The prose, to me, reads awkwardly but perseverance is rewarded with lots and lots of information.

175

The summaries of standard procedures and standard functions are each in alphabetical order. A page reference is given on the right of the page for every procedure and function summarized. The summary of syntax is "top down".

STANDARD PROCEDURES
AN UNSPECIFIED FILE NAME IMPLIES INPUT OR OUTPUT

DISPOSE ($name_{pointer}$) • return an unwanted record to the heap — 139

GET ($name_{file}$) • advance the window on the nominated input file — 125

NEW ($name_{pointer}$) • create a new and empty record — 139

PACK ($name_{loose}$, $subscript_{loose}$, $name_{tight}$) • pack the contents of one array in another — 88

PAGE ($name_{file}$) • write a form-feed character to nominated output file ⟨ if printer can respond to it ⟩ — 116

PUT ($name_{file}$) • advance the window on the nominated output file — 125

READ ($name_{file}$, variable,) • read from nominated file; items on TEXT files are separated by spaces or new lines or both — 117

READLN (($name_{file}$, variable,) / ($name_{file}$)) • as READ but only for TEXT files: skip to next line of input when the final parameter has been satisfied — 117

RESET ($name_{file}$) • prepare the nominated file for reading ⟨ never reset INPUT or rewrite OUTPUT ⟩ — 114

REWRITE ($name_{file}$) • prepare the nominated file for writing — 114

UNPACK ($name_{tight}$, $name_{loose}$, $subscript_{loose}$) • the converse of PACK — 88

WRITE ($name_{file}$, expression : width : places) — 116

WRITELN (($name_{file}$, expression : width : places) / ($name_{file}$)) — 116

• *width* and *places* are integer expressions. *places* is applicable only if the *expression* whose value is to be written is of type REAL.

STANDARD FUNCTIONS

i denotes an expression that reduces to an integer value , *r* denotes an expression reducing to a *real* value, *m* denotes a parameter which has an ordinal value: *e.g.* integer, character or member of enumerated type.

ABS(*i*)	● *absolute value* : ABS(-6) returns 6 《an integer 》	36
ABS(*r*)	● *absolute value*: ABS(-6.5) returns 6.5 《a real 》	36
ARCTAN(*r*)	● *arctangent* : ARCTAN(1.0) returns 0.785398 《 π/4 》	37
CHR(*i*)	● *character* : CHR(65) returns 'A' if code is ASCII	41
COS(*r*)	● *cosine* : COS(3.141593/3) returns 0.5	37
EOF (*name*_{file}) *INPUT implied*	● returns TRUE if READ would fail on its next attempt because of meeting end-of-file	39
EOLN (*name*_{file}) *INPUT implied*	● returns TRUE if READ would next read the space signifying an end of line	39
EXP(*r*)	● *exponent*, or *natural antilogarithm*: EXP(1) returns 2.7182818 《*i.e.* e¹ 》	36
LN(*r*)	● *natural logarithm* : LN(2.7182818) returns 1 《*i.e.* *ln*(e) 》	36
ODD(*i*)	● *odd*: ODD(-3) returns TRUE ; ODD(0) returns TRUE	39
ORD(*m*)	● *ordinal value*: ORD('A') returns 65 if ASCII code; ORD(TRUE) returns 1; ORD(FALSE) returns 0	40
PRED(*m*)	● *predecessor*: PRED('B') returns 'A' ; PRED(6) returns 5; PRED(TRUE) returns FALSE	41
ROUND(*r*)	● *round to nearest integer*: ROUND(3.5) returns 4; ROUND(-3.8) returns -4	38
SIN(*r*)	● *sine* : SIN(3.141593/6) returns 0.5	37
SQR(*i*)	● *square*: SQR(-3) returns 9 《an integer 》	36
SQR(*r*)	● *square*: SQR(-3.0) returns 9.0 《a real 》	36
SQRT(*r*)	● *square root*: SQRT(81) returns 9.0 《a real 》	36
SUCC(*m*)	● *successor*: SUCC('A') returns B; SUCC(5) returns 6; SUCC(FALSE) returns TRUE	41
TRUNC(*r*)	● *truncate to integer*: TRUNC(-3.8) returns -3 《an integer 》	38

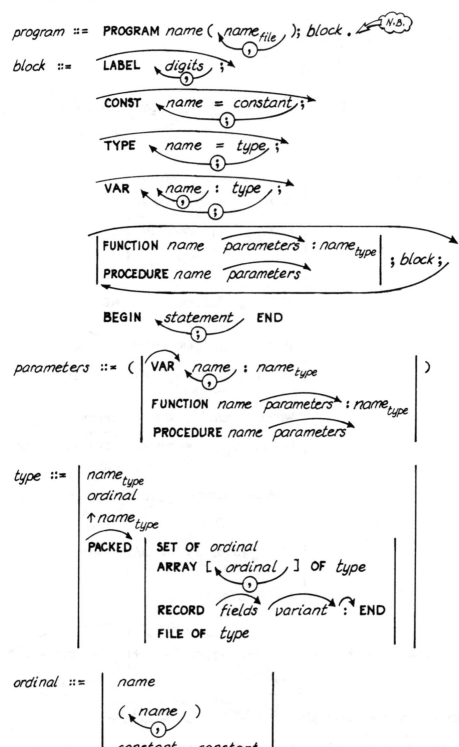

program ::= **PROGRAM** *name* (*name*$_{file}$); *block* . *N.B.*

block ::= **LABEL** *digits* ;

CONST *name* = *constant* ;

TYPE *name* = *type* ;

VAR *name* : *type* ;

FUNCTION *name* *parameters* : *name*$_{type}$

PROCEDURE *name* *parameters* ; *block* ;

BEGIN *statement* **END**

parameters ::= (**VAR** *name* : *name*$_{type}$)

FUNCTION *name* *parameters* : *name*$_{type}$

PROCEDURE *name* *parameters*

type ::= *name*$_{type}$

ordinal

↑ *name*$_{type}$

PACKED **SET OF** *ordinal*

ARRAY [*ordinal*] **OF** *type*

RECORD *fields* *variant* : **END**

FILE OF *type*

ordinal ::= *name*

(*name*)

constant .. *constant*

SYNTAX (SUMMARY CONTINUED)

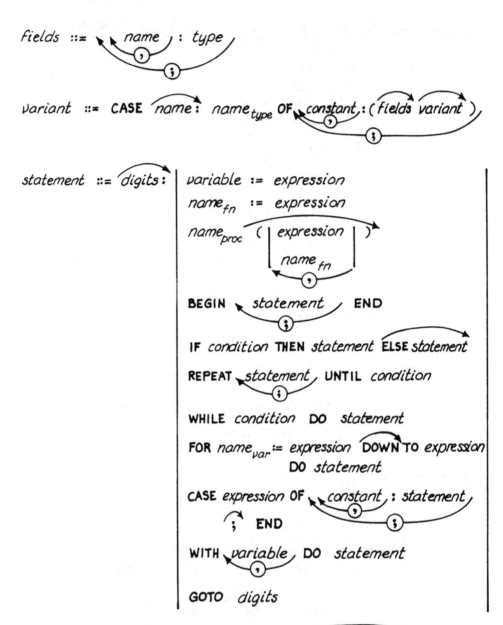

fields ::= ← _name_ : _type_ →
    (,)
    (;)

variant ::= **CASE** _name_ : _name_$_{type}$ **OF** _constant_, : (_fields variant_)
    (,)
    (;)

statement ::= _digits_ : | _variable_ := _expression_

    name$_{fn}$:= _expression_

    name$_{proc}$ (| _expression_ |)
          | _name_ $_{fn}$ |
               (,)

    BEGIN _statement_ **END**
          (;)

    IF _condition_ **THEN** _statement_ **ELSE** _statement_

    REPEAT _statement_ **UNTIL** _condition_
          (;)

    WHILE _condition_ **DO** _statement_

    FOR _name_$_{var}$:= _expression_ **DOWN TO** _expression_
          DO _statement_

    CASE _expression_ **OF** _constant_ : _statement_
          (,)   (;)
    ; **END**

    WITH _variable_ **DO** _statement_
          (,)

    GOTO _digits_

expression ::= | + | → _term_ → _comparator_ | + | → _term_ →
       | − | (_operator_) | − | (_operator_)

condition ::= _expression_ ← (_reducing to Boolean value_)

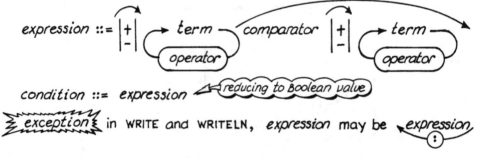

≋_exception_≋ in **WRITE** and **WRITELN**, _expression_ may be _expression_
                                                              (:)

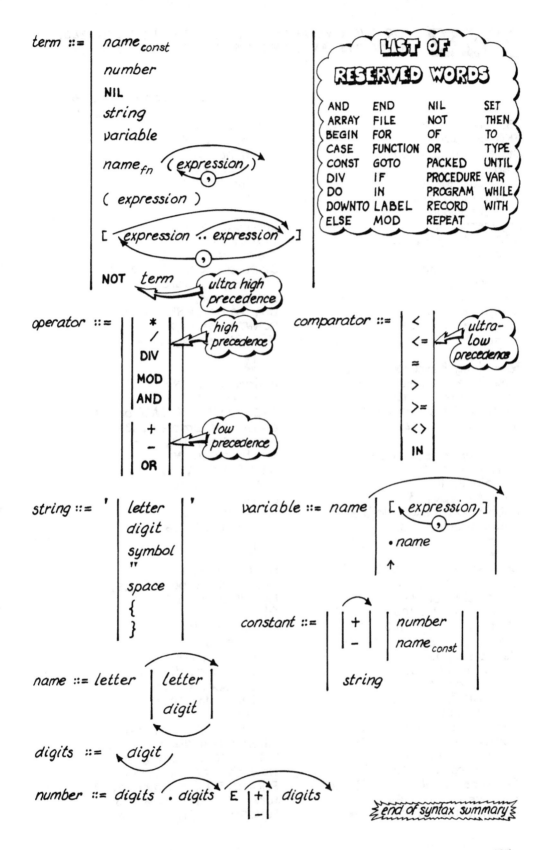